The MORBID CURIOUS

The MORBID CURIOUS NO.4

The MORBID CURIOUS

Journal of Ghosts, Murder and the Macabre

No. 4

Annual Samhain Edition!

Welcome to our First Anniversary Issue! It was one year ago that we launched our first Halloween issue of the Morbid Curious and now we're back again with a special issue "Among the Spirits!"

It's interesting how this issue came about for me because it contains at article that was not supposed to be there in the first place. In keeping with the initial theme, we had several writers contribute stories about Spiritualism and the Spirit World and as I was putting them together, I realized that all the contributors for this issue were women. That turned out to be a bit ironic considering that Spiritualism in the nineteenth century offered American women the first chance to strike out independently on their own, becoming mediums, and important figures in the movement. Many believe that Spiritualism contributed greatly to the founding of women's rights in our country, so it only seemed fitting that as the only man in the issue, I write a piece on how women not only created the Spiritualist movement but were the reason it existed for as long as it did. The paranormal field that we have today would not exist if not for the women who made it great - and neither would this issue!

I hope you enjoy it!

Troy Taylor

Autumnal Equinox 2021

TABLE OF CONTENTS

What Do the Spirits Have For You in This Issue?

EDITOR AND ART DIRECTOR
Troy Taylor

COVER ART DESIGNER
April Slaughter

CONTACT
ghosts@americanhauntings.net

This Book is Published By:
American Hauntings Ink
Jacksonville, Illinois | 217.791.7859
Visit us on the Internet at http://www.americanhauntingsink.com

First Edition - October 2021

Printed in the United States of America

THE KNOCKING DEAD

The Start of America's Love Affair with the Spirit World

TROY TAYLOR

SPIRITUALISM GALVANIZED AMERICAN SOCIETY FOR NEARLY A CENTURY, FASCINATING PEOPLE FROM EVERY WALK OF LIFE. IT WAS FOUNDED ON THE BELIEF THAT LIFE EXISTED AFTER DEATH AND THAT THE SPIRIT COULD CONTINUE TO EXIST OUTSIDE OF THE BODY. MOST IMPORTANTLY, SPIRITUALISTS MAINTAINED THAT THESE SPIRITS COULD — AND DID — COMMUNICATE WITH THE LIVING.

The Fox sisters have long been regarded as the founders of the Spiritualist movement in America. I know that I have given them credit for it on more than one occasion over the years, even though, in truth, that's not really accurate. They weren't the first to contact the spirit world in America, but they were certainly the ones who made it popular.

A belief in the spirit world has existed in every time period and in every part of the world. Ghosts have been one of man's enduring fascinations, dating all the way back to the Stone Age, when people began burying the dead with ceremonies that were intended to ensure that the soul of the deceased rested in peace. A belief in disembodied spirits can be found in ancient writings from the Babylonians, Sumerians, Assyrians, and Egyptians. Every culture had stories of ghosts and even the Bible contained the story about a witch who communicated with the spirit of the prophet Samuel.

Those who settled along the eastern seaboard of the United States brought with them their customs and beliefs from their homelands. In the bellies of ships, packed right next to their belongings, were stories of witches, monsters, and the restless dead. America already had its own legends and places of mystery when the first colonists arrived, and the new stories mixed with he old to create a melting pot of the supernatural in the forests, hills, and mountains of New England and beyond.

It was only a matter of time before someone started talking to the creatures that were hiding out among the trees and wandering endlessly among the old houses, crumbling stones, and graveyards of the region.

And Maggie and Kate Fox became the people to do so.

"HERE, MR. SPLITFOOT..."

In December of 1847, John and Margaret Fox, along with their two daughters, into a small wooden-frame house in the village of Hydesville, New York, which was really just a group of homes, several small stores and mills, and typical of other small farm communities scattered across the northwest part of the state.

The cottage in Hydesville where the Fox family lived during the winter of 1847-1848.

Legends say that the house was haunted before the Fox family came to live there. Those in the neighborhood often referred to it as "the spook house." Between 1843 and 1844, a couple named Bell occupied the cottage. In the last few months of their occupancy, a young local woman named Lucretia Pulver handled the household chores. She acted as a maid and carried out the cleaning and cooking duties for the Bells.

The story that Lucretia would later tell claimed that a peddler came to the door of the house one day with a case of merchandise. The friendly young man offered goods for sale like pots, pans, cutlery, and other items for the kitchen. He stayed with the family for several days and it has been suggested that perhaps he enjoyed a closer than was proper relationship with Mrs. Bell. With no explanation, Lucretia was told that her services would no longer be required by the Bells. Saddened, but understanding, the young woman gathered her things, pausing only long enough to purchase a small kitchen knife from the peddler. He offered to deliver the knife to her father's farm, but then he never showed up with it.

Barely a week later, Lucretia was surprised to find that Mrs. Bell was again requesting her services. Thankful to have her job back, she reported for duty the next morning. The peddler who had been staying with the family had departed but she found that many of the items that he had been selling were now in the Bell home. Lucretia assumed that the items had been purchased from the peddler before he left and thought no more about it. Nothing seemed out of the ordinary about the house, but that was soon to change.

Soon after returning to work, Lucretia noticed some particularly strange things were occurring. She heard unaccountable knocking and tapping sounds in the walls and, on several occasions, heard footsteps walking about the house and descending the stairs to the cellar. The house was empty at the time. Lucretia began to feel uneasy when left in the house alone. She would often send for her brother, or a friend, to come and stay with her and usually, the strange sounds would cease. However, on one occasion, they continued for hours and scared Lucretia's brother so badly that

Leah Fish was nearly two decades older than her younger sisters and would manipulate herself into their lives and control their finances for years.

he left the house and refused to return. Lucretia didn't work there much longer. The Bells moved away, and the young woman was soon out of a job again.

She never expected to enter the cottage again but soon, odd happenings would bring her back to its front door.

The Fox family should have never been in the cottage. John had purchased some nearby land but there was a delay in getting a home built on the property. Forced to find a temporary place to stay, he rented the cottage in Hydesville. Their stay in the cottage would turn out to be an eventful one.

John and Margaret were both past 50 in 1848. Their two daughters - Margaretta, who went by Maggie, and Catherine, who was known as Kate - were 7-and 10-years old. They were pretty girls with dark hair and eyes. There were also older siblings who were married and lived on their own. A son, David, lived nearby with his family, as did a sister, Maria. One daughter, Elizabeth, lived in Canada with her husband. Leah, the oldest of the Fox siblings, was a piano teacher and lived in Rochester, which was about 30 miles away. She was two decades older than her two youngest sisters, but she did have a daughter, Lizzie, who was close in age to Maggie and Kate, and she spent as much time with them as she did at home.

Leah will become a problematic figure in this story, as she also was in the lives of her little sisters. In 1827, when Leah was just 14, she had married a driftless man named Bowman Fish. Their marriage was short, and Fish left town and was never seen again. Leah's only reminder her marriage was Lizzie - and her poverty. With no husband to support her, she taught piano to put food on the table. But Leah's circumstances - like the lives of all the Fox family - were about to change.

Hydesville was not much of a town and fittingly, the cottage was not much of a home. It was small, but serviceable, with several windows and two stoves to keep away the cold of the upstate New York nights. The front door opened directly into the south-facing parlor. The kitchen was on the northwest side and had its own door to the yard. On the east side, a pantry - sometimes used as a second bedroom - connected to the kitchen, and the main bedroom adjoined the parlor. An enclosed staircase between the pantry and the main bedroom led up to a large attic, and another staircase led down to the cellar. The house was located on the busy corner of Hydesville and Parker Roads, which would make it easy to find

for the scores of people who came to see if the stories they heard about the strange activities occurring there were true.

The cottage was an unlikely place for the birth of an enormous national movement that would attract millions of people and dramatically change the way that Americans would come to view life and death. But it was in that small house, in that small town, where Spiritualism began on a cold March night in 1848.

America would never be the same again.

Things were quiet for the first three months that the Foxes lived in their rented home. Soon, though, neighbors began telling them of the cottage's "spooky" reputation for "mysterious rapping noises." The family tried to ignore the tales because they were already experiencing the strange happenings for themselves. The noises became worse toward the end of the winter. The banging and rattling sounds pounded loudly each night, disturbing them all from their sleep.

John Fox, not a superstitious man, assumed the noises that frightened his wife and children were merely the sounds of an unfamiliar dwelling, amplified by active imaginations. But he

An illustration of the chaos taking place in the Fox house after Kate and Maggie began making contact with the spirits believed to be haunting the place.

John's wife, Margaret, was convinced that supernatural events were occurring in the house. She believed it was haunted by an "unhappy, restless spirit."

Even Mrs. Fox swore that she had heard disembodied footsteps walking through the house and then going down the wooden steps into the dank cellar. John searched for every possible explanation for the sounds but could find nothing.

Margaret Fox had her own explanation for the happenings - there was an "unhappy restless spirit" haunting the place.

On the evening of March 31, John began his nightly ritual of investigating the house for the source of the sounds. He thoroughly searched the cottage; he was no closer to finding the source of the mysterious tappings. Then, Kate began to realize that whenever her father knocked on a wall or doorframe, the same number of inexplicable knocks would come in reply.

It was as if someone, or something, was trying to communicate with them.

Finding her nerve, Kate spoke up, addressing the unseen presence by the nickname that she and her sister had given it. "Here, Mr. Splitfoot," she called out, "Do as I do!"

She clapped her hands together two times and seconds later, two knocks

wasn't so sure about that after Kate woke up screaming one night, saying that a cold hand had touched her on the face. Maggie swore that invisible hands had pulled the blankets from her bed.

came in reply, seemingly from inside of the wall. She followed this display by rapping on the table and the precise number of knocks came again from the presence. The activity caught the attention of the rest of the family, and they entered the room with Kate and her father. Margaret Fox tried asking aloud questions of fact, such as the ages of her daughters. To her surprise, each reply was eerily accurate.

Unsure of what to do, John summoned several neighbors to the house to observe the phenomenon. The first was Mrs. Mary Redfield, who was blunt and dismissive about the presence of a spirit and assumed the girls were playing a prank. She quickly changed her mind. After questioning the spirit and receiving correct answer to her inquiries, she became frightened and left the house.

One neighbor, William Duesler, decided to try and communicate with the source of the sounds in a more scientific manner. He asked repeated questions and created a form of alphabet using a series of knocks. He also determined the number of knocks that could be interpreted as "yes" and "no." In such a manner, he divined the subject of the disturbances. The secret of the haunting came out, not in private, but before an assembled group of witnesses. The presence in the house claimed that it was the spirit of a peddler who had been murdered and robbed years before.

As it happened, one of the neighbors who came to the house was the former maid, Lucretia Pulver. She told the story of the peddler who came to the Bell house one day and never left. John Fox and William Duesler went to the cellar and began to dig. It took them more than an hour, but they managed to unearth some scraps of clothing and a small piece of human skull with strands of hair still clinging to it. A local doctor determined that someone had been buried there and that charcoal and quicklime had been used to hasten the body's decay. The Foxes and their neighbors became convinced that the presence in the house was that of the murdered peddler.

Soon, news of the spirit rappings attracted so much attention that a great many visitors began showing up at the Fox home, many of them demanding entry, numbering up to 500 people in a single day. Mr. Fox complained: "It caused a great deal of trouble and anxiety. I am not a believer in haunted houses or supernatural appearances." But John could not account for the noises, or for the other manifestations that began to occur. Door slammed, beds shook, footsteps paced back and forth and down the stairs to the cellar, and the rapping sounds continued to be heard. By early April, the sounds were heard both day and night.

The startling stories about the Fox house quickly spread throughout the region and beyond. The events attracted curiosity from both believers and skeptics. This was no mere ghost story. The Fox sisters and an alleged unseen entity had established a communication network that was unlike anything people had heard about before. The story touched a nerve among a population that was eager to look beyond the limits of ordinary life and ponder the mystery of what came next.

Within a matter of months, what began in Hydesville spread to surrounding communities, and from there, via newspapers, to the large cities. There was no way to explain why this one particular event so vividly captured the imagination of the public. It was as if people suddenly found confirmation of the spirit world's ability to communicate with the physical world.

AMERICA'S FIRST MEDIUMS

As the public became more and more fascinated by the rappings at the Hydesville house, it was decided that Kate and Maggie should be sent to stay with their older sister, Leah, in Rochester. This may have had the opposite effect to that intended by the girls' parents, for the rapping sounds followed them to Rochester. In this much larger town, the Fox sisters attracted even more attention. Kate was soon sent to Auburn to stay with her brother in hopes that she would be free from the harassment of the knockings, but Maggie became the center of a devoted "spirit circle," which allowed participants to come together to receive spirit communications. The circle worked out a more manageable code to communicate with the spirits: one rap indicated "no," two raps that the spirit was unable to answer a question, and three raps meant "yes."

As many enthusiastic residents of Rochester made it a nightly occurrence to gather at Leah's home to witness the wonderful revelations that Maggie produced from the spirit world, Leah began doing the math and realized that she was sitting on a fortune.

About that, Leah was correct. She had lived near poverty for years and now she realized she had a way out of her circumstances - and she would do so thanks to the hunger of the masses for what her little sisters could offer.

The state of New York was buzzing with news of the spirits. It had only been a few years since Samuel Morse had first successfully demonstrated the miracle of the telegraph. If electricity could provide instant communication between distant places, why then wasn't contact possible between the living and the dead? Perhaps the marvel of electricity played some role in spirit contact, some suggested, and the term "rapping telegraph" began to be heard.

However, Rochester - like many other towns in the area - was sharply divided about the reality of what was taking place in Leah's home. While Maggie had many supporters, there were some, especially Christian fundamentalists, who denounced the girl for "heresy" and "blasphemy." Leah knew she had to change people's minds if she was going to build a fortune using Maggie's talents.

She cleverly arranged a public lecture and demonstration so that everyone could see for themselves. The event was held at Corinthian Hall, the city's largest auditorium, and the admission was the steep price of $1 per

News of the Fox Sisters and the strange events in their home began to spread - first on a local level, then nationally, which was unheard of during this time in American history.

person. The audience was made up of a wide range of people, from the simply curious to those who believed they were witnesses to a spiritual revolution in the making, and they filled the hall to capacity. With a sold-out crowd of more than 400, Leah profited handsomely, while Maggie's career as a medium was launched.

Of those who attended the demonstration that night, many were

Committees were formed to try and determine if there was a fraudulent cause for the mysterious rappings, but every committee went away disappointed.

Disappointed, the debunkers formed a second committee, which would announce a solution later on - but when that date came, they also declared that they had been unable to detect any trickery. A doctor had even listened to Maggie with a stethoscope to rule out ventriloquism, all to no effect.

More public demonstrations followed. Public opinion in Rochester became even more heated. A third committee was formed and one of its members swore publicly that if he could not discover how the raps were made, he would throw himself over Genesee Falls. Hopefully, this man's friends were able to dissuade him from such a course of action because the third committee had no more luck than the previous two. Though some of its members were privately certain that spirits did not cause the raps, the third committee, like the others, was forced to admit that it couldn't tell how the sounds were being accomplished.

certain they had witnessed genuine spirit communication, while others were just as sure they had witnessed a fraud. If the skeptics of the city expected to witness a public exposure of fraud in return for their dollar, they were sorely disappointed because no one could explain what caused the rappings. A committee of leading citizens reported itself completely unable to give a natural explanation for the rappings, which each of them had heard.

At the last demonstration at Corinthian Hall, the audience became so frustrated that a disturbance broke out. Amid angry shouts and threats, a squad of police arrived to break up the meeting and was forced to escort Maggie and Leah home to protect them from the indignant mob.

But the Fox sisters were just about to outgrow Rochester, New York. Kate rejoined her sister, and the two girls quickly began receiving publicity from throughout the state. While Kate had lived in Auburn, she had not been idle. She had also conducted séances there and had her own believers flocking to join her spirit circle. It wasn't long before news of their demonstrations was being reported in much larger cities, and the girls were becoming nationally known, which was unusual in an era when such celebrity was rare.

Within a few months later, with their popularity still surging, they began traveling around the country, appearing in a variety of venues. The publicity around them was intense. Some newspapers and public venues hailed them as frauds and others as sensations. Regardless, people flocked to see them in massive numbers, all of them gladly paying for the privilege. They toured the country, becoming hugely popular and their séances became more elaborate, with objects moving about, spirits appearing, and tables levitating. They also gave private demonstrations for those customers who could afford them.

The Age of Spiritualism had begun and was already generating money. Skeptics, to their dismay, were powerless to curb the enthusiasm of hundreds of thousands of people who sought contact with the spirit world. There was a sudden demand for mediums, and although the Fox sisters were there first, they soon had competition that would force them to fight for a place in an increasingly crowded market. Other mediums were soon breaking into the scene for their share of the limelight.

When the girls had first appeared on the scene, they were lauded by believers, who saw their gifts as blessings from the spirit world. Of course, not everyone felt that way. They were also slammed by skeptics and detractors --who actually did the sisters the greatest favor. Since the girls could not easily be exposed as frauds, most people concluded that they must be genuine. It also didn't hurt that Maggie and Kate were both young and attractive. The sisters were embraced by such celebrities as P.T. Barnum, William Cullen Bryant, Harriet Beecher Stowe, James Fenimore Cooper, and newspaper editor Horace Greeley, who provided quarters for the girls at his home.

Greeley and his wife had lost four of their five children and when he met the girls, he was still grieving over the

Newspaper publisher Horace Greeley was a great supporter of the Fox sisters.

After he witnessed the "rapping phenomena" several times, under what he described as "test conditions," he pronounced himself perplexed by what he saw. He wasted no time in writing an editorial in the *New York Tribune* titled "The Mysterious Rappings." Greeley said that he believed the raps were genuine, if inexplicable, but initially had doubts that spirits were responsible. He later changed his mind and there is no question that Greeley's support for the Fox sisters did a great deal to boost their fame and credibility, as well as that of the entire Spiritualist movement.

recent death of his son. The possibility that the dead might be still accessible to the living was of great interest to him.

P.T. Barnum, that sensational showman, read and enjoyed news accounts of the Fox Sisters' powers and he offered to feature them at his American Museum. The building was a

P.T. Barnum, with one of his most famous attractions - General Tom Thumb - and his famous American Museum, where the Fox sisters performed, drawing huge crowds.

marble showcase on Lower Broadway in New York City, decorated with blazing flags and packed with more than 600,000 living and dead curiosities -- from stuffed animals to fortune-tellers, to three-legged men and bearded ladies. The

First Lady Jane Pierce and her son, Benjamin, whose death she was never able to recover from. She would invite the Fox Sisters to the White House.

pretty Fox Sisters became quite an attraction. They were shy, barely educated, and simply dressed in neat dark frocks with white collars, but quickly attracted a crowd. Barnum was sure that guests would sit down with the girls who talked to the dead and he was right. Regular admission to the American Museum was 25-cents but to converse with ghosts, people might pay as much as a dollar or even more.

The Fox sisters became so famous that their reputations brought them all the way to the White House.

On January 6, 1853, only two months before Franklin Pierce was to be inaugurated as America's fourteenth president, tragedy struck he and his wife, Jane. The Pierces were traveling by train with their only child, Benjamin, 11, and the car they were traveling in became uncoupled and derailed. The train tumbled, split apart and crashed down a rocky ledge. President-elect and Mrs. Pierce suffered only minor injuries. There was only one death in the crash - young Benjamin Pierce, whose head was struck by a large rock, crushing his skull while his parents helplessly watched.

For the frail Jane Pierce, witnessing her son's horrible death was so traumatic that she never recovered emotionally. She was inconsolable for weeks and so paralyzed by grief that she was unable to attend her husband's inauguration in March 1853. Benjamin's death cast a pall over their life and over the presidency. Jane became one of the most tragic figures to ever occupy the White House. She remained there in solitude, writing lengthy letters to her dead son, whom she never stopped mourning.

Aching for contact with her son's spirit, she wrote to the Fox sisters, who were receiving national publicity as Spiritualism swept the nation. The two young mediums were invited to a séance at the White House, where they would attempt to receive spirit raps from Benjamin in the next world. Exactly what occurring during this séance is unknown, for no records exist to say what messages were given to Mrs. Pierce. The sisters never revealed any details about their White House experience, but rumors circulated that it was successful.

FAME, GLORY, AND A FALL FROM GRACE

Even though most major American newspapers branded Spiritualism a fraud and a swindle, but a huge number of Americans weren't listening. What they preferred to hear was a message coming from parents, aunts, uncles, cousins and children in the next world.

But that wasn't the case with everyone. Many were not as convinced by the sisters as Greeley, Cooper, and the Pierces had been. The Fox sisters were routinely exposed by skeptics as

fakes and it was claimed they produced their phenomena in a variety of ways ranging from toe, knee, and ankle cracking to ventriloquism, to assorted mechanical devices. Despite these accusations, though, no trickery was ever discovered. Dozens of committees and forums were created to test the powers of the sisters. Most involved posing questions to the spirits and while the replies were often inconsistent, they were accurate enough to make an impression. One test involved the girls being bound tightly about the ankles so that they could not move their feet. Even trussed up, they still managed to produce eerie rapping sounds. A committee of women also checked the girl's undergarments to ensure that nothing was hidden there to produce the sounds. They found nothing and despite the hostility shown to the sisters by the committees, the members were forced to admit that they were unable to detect fraud.

Even so, some of the accounts of the sister's methods and activities are troubling. Leah was often accused of trying to glean personal information from the sitters at the séances that would help the "spirits" to give out correct answers. They also excelled at calling on the spirits of the famous dead. The results of this were not

LEAH   KATE   MARGARETTA

Although frequently criticized by skeptics and the press, this did little to dampen the public enthusiasm for the sisters. They made so much money from their performances that Leah became a "medium," too. She also controlled the finances of her sisters, taking a percentage as their "manager" and leaving them with only enough money to live on.

always impressive. When one sitter noted that Benjamin Franklin's spirit seemed to be surprisingly lacking in good grammar, Maggie Fox stomped away from the séance table with only the reply of, "You know I never understood grammar!" As dubious as the séances may have been, though, thousands were convinced that the girls were genuine, and business boomed.

In March 1850, yet another committee was formed and this one managed to offer a solid opinion about how the girls could be "creating" the rapping phenomena. The members of the committee, all professors of medicine, sat on the floor in a soundproof room for an hour while firmly holding onto Maggie's legs. It was a rather undignified way for three gentlemen to pass the time with a young and unmarried girl in those days, but they tackled the task with great fervor. According to their report, they were rewarded for effort. It was noted that the spirits only chose to make themselves heard when one of the investigators was forced to relax his hands a little bit from fatigue. The committee stated that, in the opinion of the investigators, Maggie's knee joints made the spirit rappings. It was suggested that she had the ability to snap these joints in much the same way that some people can crack their knuckles. She accomplished this, the investigators believed, without any visible motion, however.

Shortly after the committee report became public, the Fox sisters - especially Leah -- issued immediate denials. She asserted that there had been few rappings during the investigation because the "friendly spirits had retired when they witnessed the harsh proceedings of the persecutors." Leah's defensiveness was understandable, since she stood to lose her share of what had become a thriving business, but what was more remarkable was the way that many prominent people sprang to Maggie's defense. The accusations were untrue, they insisted, simply because they could not be true! Everyone knew that spirits existed, so why in the world would Maggie use her knee joints to imitate their rappings?

The popularity of the sisters was barely affected by the criticisms. In 1853, the sisters demonstrated what was described as "their most powerful early manifestations." It consisted of a table levitating with a well-known politician, Governor George Talmadge, seated on top of it. Talmadge also claimed that he'd received a message through spirit writing from the ghost of another notable political figure, John C. Calhoun.

Soon after, though, the sensation began to fade. For one thing, the public wanted more exciting spirit demonstrations than mere rappings and the girls were facing competition from many other mediums, even as the skeptics continued their attacks on them.

Later in their lives, Kate and Maggie fell on hard times. They had suffered through years of séances, public appearances, tours, tests, and scrutiny, much of it antagonistic. Those who knew the sisters felt they had been physically and emotionally drained by their grueling schedule. They simply were not sophisticated enough to understand when they were young that they were being exploited by their older sister, their promoters, and their desperate audiences. Nor did they fully comprehend the depth and hostility of the religious and scientific controversy that surrounded Spiritualism. They were the first to venture professionally into the new movement, and each paid the price for it.

Maggie abandoned mediumship for love. In Philadelphia, she met and fell in love with famed Arctic explorer Elisha Kent Kane, the dashing son of an aristocratic family, who did not deem

Maggie worthy of marrying into their line. They did exchange vows and rings in the company of friends but were never legally wed. Unfortunately, the affair ended in tragedy when Kane died in 1857. Maggie was left broken-hearted and almost penniless. She had abandoned being a medium but now had to take it up again. She began drinking and her health and her mental state began to decline.

Leah, who in addition to taking advantage of her younger sisters also began practicing as a medium, married for a third time in 1858 to Daniel Underhill, a successful insurance man. Leah, like Maggie, withdrew from Spiritualism for a time.

Kate, however, continued her career. In 1861, she went to work as a medium for wealthy New York banker Charles Livermore. His wife, Estelle, had died the previous year. Over the next five years, Kate provided the banker with close to 400 séances in his home. There were many witnesses to the sittings and written documentation was kept. Eventually, at the 43rd sitting, the spirit of Estelle Livermore "materialized" and was seen surrounded by what was described as a "psychic light." The spirit communicated to Kate via rappings and automatic writing. According to accounts, Estelle and

Maggie gave up being a spirit medium when she married arctic explorer Elisha Kent Kane. When he died in 1857, she was left penniless and returned to the spirit world, which drove her to madness and drink.

another spirit, calling himself Benjamin Franklin, wrote on cards before Livermore. While Estelle was writing, Kate's hands were held tight. Witnesses claimed that the script on the card was the perfect reproduction of Estelle's earthly handwriting.

Finally, during the 338th séance, Estelle made it known that she would no longer materialize. True to this communication, Livermore never saw his late wife's spirit again. But because he was grateful to Kate for the comfort that she had brought him in his grief, he paid for her journey to England in 1871

Kate continued her mediumship as an adult, married and English barrister, and had two sons. But eventually, her life would also fall apart, just like Maggie's did.

so that she could continue her work as a medium.

In England, her career thrived, and she often gave sittings for well-known figures of the day. Kate also made herself available for testing by British scientists like Sir William Crookes, one of the greatest physicists of his time and one of the first advocates for serious inquiry into the paranormal. She also shared several séances with the famed mediums of the era, Daniel Dunglas Home and Agnes Guppy-Volckman.

She remained in England and the following year, married Henry Jencken, a barrister, with whom she had two sons. Her reputation as a medium earned Kate a visit to Russia in 1883, where she demonstrated her gifts for the czar.

There was a lesson to be learned by Kate's rise to stardom in Europe and by her earlier employment by men like Charles Livermore. It was a lesson that was overlooked by many scientists, clergy, intellectuals, and rational thinkers in their zeal to debunk and expose Spiritualism as a fraud. The fact was that millions of people, just like Livermore and Jane Pierce, regardless of their social or economic status, were seeking a way to cope with death and the grief that followed. Spiritualism, for all its flaws, fakes, and frauds, offered a connection between this world and the afterlife. The spirit world offered hope that death was not the end and that we would be reunited with our loved ones in the next world. Many scientists, skeptics, and rationalists never quite grasped the value of Spiritualism and the need that it fulfilled for so many people. Nor could they understand that their cold logic failed to offer anything that could ease the fear and mystery of death.

Like it or not, Spiritualism in the nineteenth century produced a critical shift in the way that Americans thought about life and death. Promising mediums had emerged and many of those who investigated them, including some of the most learned men in the country, concluded that there was evidence to make a case for communication with discarnate spirits.

For both the dying and the bereaved, Spiritualism offered something more tangible than unyielding and often impersonal religious dogma, which is why it attracted people from everyone church denomination across America. Although fundamentalist clergy strongly disapproved of it, many people found that the message and hope of Spiritualism was very similar to Christian teachings. In many places in the New Testament, the Bible spoke of eternal life, the same belief that the Spiritualists espoused about the afterlife. However, traditional Christianity would continue to preach against Spiritualists, reminding the faithful that the Old Testament condemned any association with mediums, fortune-tellers, necromancers, and the like.

Americans in the nineteenth century had a much closer contact with death than recent and present-day generations. More people died at home. Life expectancy in the nineteenth century was much shorter than it is today. Infections, epidemics, and unsophisticated medical treatments claimed many lives. Families had large numbers of children because high infant mortality rates, accidents, and childhood diseases claimed the lives of so many infants and toddlers.

When the Fox sisters were growing up, death was not an unusual topic, even in public schools. Schoolbooks, songs, and poems featured accounts of dying children and by today's standards, seem morbid and inappropriate for young children to read in class. But death was ever-present in the nineteenth century and making sure children were prepared for it, even at an early age, was both practical and responsible on the part of parents, schools, and churches. When the Civil War came along, Americans saw wholesale slaughter in numbers that could never have been imagined before. With all this death, it was no surprise that Spiritualism was instantly popular when it arrived on the scene. It added a measure of comfort and acceptance of death and offered hope of what awaited us when we left our physical body.

In 1876, Maggie Fox visited England for a time and then returned home to the United States. She was still

The three Fox sisters later in life, just before their falling out. Kate and Maggie would eventually patch things up but they never spoke to Leah again.

a medium, albeit a reluctant one, forced to continue practicing because of her dire economic situation. Those who knew her recalled that she lived in poverty during her last years.

Then, the lives of the Fox sisters took another unhappy turn. While the reasons remain unclear, the three of them became embroiled in quarrels and disputes with one another that were apparently instigated by Maggie. Their later years were mired in public controversy and personal difficulties, not the least of which was alcohol and a lack of funds. Only Leah had ever prospered from the talents of her younger sisters.

By 1885, Spiritualism was on the decline and investigations of fraud began to increase. This year brought further tragedy to the Fox sisters. Maggie performed before a commission in New York to prove her skills -- a test

that she failed miserably -- and Kate suffered the death of her husband from a stroke. She returned to New York and there, in early 1888, she was arrested for drunkenness and idleness and welfare workers took custody of her sons. Maggie, in a moment of kindness for a sister with whom she had been feuding, was unable to get the boys herself but she did manage to get them into the custody of an uncle in England.

In 1888, Spiritualism was dealt a savage blow that sent it reeling. On October 21, Maggie took part in a lecture and demonstration that has become an infamous event in the history of the Spiritualist movement. On this night, at the New York Academy of Music, she denounced Spiritualism as a complete and total sham. The years of alcohol abuse, loneliness, and grief had taken their toll on her, and she weighed the idea of committing suicide before finally choosing confession instead. She walked out on stage to announce that she and Kate had created the strange rappings heard in their Hydesville home by simply cracking their toes. She also stated that Leah had forced them into performing as mediums for the public.

She reportedly told the audience: "I have seen so much miserable deception. That is why I am willing to state that Spiritualism is a fraud of the worst description... It is the greatest sorrow of my life. I began the deception when I was too young to know right from wrong."

Devoted Spiritualists denounced Maggie's confession as the ravings of a sad and tired drunk. Kate, who did not speak at the public appearance, later stated that she did not agree with her sister, and she continued to perform as a medium. It was also publicly argued by various individuals and groups that Maggie had been forced into a false confession by churches or had been bribed by the newspapers. It was also pointed out, a little more reasonably, that the existence of one fraudulent medium did not prove that all others were not genuine. Some even claimed that Maggie did not know her own powers and was a true medium, despite what she may have thought about herself.

There was also an alternate theory that later emerged to explain the confession. After Maggie had stepped into help Kate with her children, the two sisters mended fences and began battling with Leah. Tensions were high and the younger sisters blamed Leah

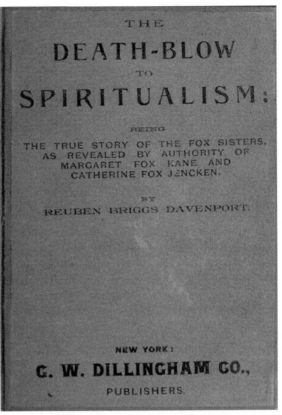

THE

DEATH-BLOW
TO
SPIRITUALISM:

BEING

THE TRUE STORY OF THE FOX SISTERS,
AS REVEALED BY AUTHORITY OF
MARGARET FOX KANE AND
CATHERINE FOX JENCKEN.

BY

REUBEN BRIGGS DAVENPORT.

NEW YORK:

G. W. DILLINGHAM CO.,
PUBLISHERS.

The cover of a book that was written that detailed Maggie's "confession" about the spirit rappings in Hydesville. She later recanted her confession, but the damage had been done to her credibility - even though it never really harmed Spiritualism itself.

for their problems - and there were plenty of problems. Maggie and Kate were nearly penniless alcoholics and resented Leah for good reason. Married three times, Leah had profited nicely from a career that she had built at the expense of her sisters. It had been Leah who had accused Kate of being an unfit mother and had her children taken away. The result of all this anger was

THE CONFESSION AND THE RETRACTION DID NOTHING FOR MAGGIE'S CAREER. THE PUBLIC WAS ANGRY, INDIGNANT, AND CONFUSED. THE PUBLISHER ISAAC FUNK, WHO KNEW THE SISTERS, REMARKED AT THE TIME ABOUT MAGGIE, "FOR FIVE DOLLARS SHE WOULD HAVE DENIED HER MOTHER, AND WOULD HAVE SWORN TO ANYTHING."

an alleged plan between Maggie and Kate to ruin Leah -- a plan that became even darker when Kate, possibly to ruin Leah's reputation, decided to join Maggie and support her confession by making one of her own. However, she never had the chance to make the confession public.

The convoluted story soon became stranger. In early 1889, Maggie recanted her confession. She explained that the financial pressures she faced were responsible for her temporary disavowal of Spiritualism. She also implied that influence from certain groups who were hostile to the subject, likely churches, forced her into the erroneous confession. The obvious implication was that Maggie and Kate would be paid to say that the spirit rappings were a hoax. Now, in her retraction, she said the opposite. Some historians have suggested that the sisters had been promised a sum of money to renounce Spiritualism but when they were never paid, they were forced to return to being mediums to

eke out a meager living. We may never know for sure.

The confession and the retraction did nothing for Maggie's career. The public was angry, indignant, and confused. But both Maggie and Kate were plagued by poverty, alcoholism, loneliness, and a variety of serious physical and emotional problems, so the turmoil that surrounded them probably didn't matter as much as it once might have. The publisher Isaac Funk, who knew the sisters, remarked at the time about Maggie, "For five dollars she would have denied her mother, and would have sworn to anything."

For debunkers, the confession had been the news they had been waiting for. They were elated that Maggie claimed the rappings were her own creation and not the work of the supernatural. Her hardships, alcoholism, and mental illness meant nothing to them.

In the end, the confession really didn't mean much either. It should have been a crippling blow to the credibility of Spiritualism, but it came too late to destroy a movement that had captivated the country for four decades. Spiritualism was not dead, much to the frustration of its enemies. The Spiritualists simply rallied their forces and continued on.

The controversy came near the end of Kate and Maggie's struggling careers. Leah, on the other hand, lived well until the end of her life. She was the first of the sisters to die, in 1890. Neither Maggie nor Kate attended her funeral. The other Fox sisters both died tragically, having been largely abandoned by those whose fortunes they had created with the birth of the Spiritualist movement. Kate drank herself to death in July 1892 at the age of only 56. Her body was discovered by one of her sons.

Maggie died in March 1893, at age 59. She spent her final days bedridden in a friend's tenement apartment in Brooklyn. She was attended by a female physician named Dr. Mellen. The doctor was not a Spiritualist, which makes her observations about Maggie's last minutes even more curious. Dr. Mellen said that during Maggie's last hours of life, there was a series of loud raps in the room. The tiny apartment contained no hiding places, not even a closet. In addition, Maggie was nearly paralyzed; she could move neither her arms nor legs. When the doctor asked about the noises, Maggie replied in a quiet, labored voice, "It was my friends watching over me." A few minutes later, she died.

THE BIRTH OF THE MOVEMENT

The story of the Fox sisters is a tale that must be told to explain the rise of a belief system that captured the attention of a nation, although, to this day, opinions still vary as to the veracity of the Fox sisters' rappings.

But the significance of the Fox sisters' story goes far beyond whether or not the women were genuine mediums. The importance of their story is the fact that Spiritualism became a massive movement in American history and attracted millions of believers, from common homes to the White House. It happened because of those two young girls, who either communicated with a spirit or managed to scare their parents with rappings noises one cold night.

If they were frauds, no one has explained how they so successfully perpetrated a hoax for so many years. Could the rappings have been carried out by trickery? Of course, that was a possibility. But many questions remain unanswered so no one can say with any certainty what actually occurred in

The Fox sisters, whether real or frauds, ushered in a new era in American history, changing the face of the nation as we know it today. Not only did millions of people become followers of the movement, but they also openly embraced the idea of life after death. Spiritualism changed everyday life, politics, and even American religion - and its impact remains today.

those theaters, opera houses, meeting halls, and private residences where they performed. Perhaps the sisters really did contact the spirits. Or perhaps they manifested psychic abilities, like psychokinesis, that allowed them to make sounds and move objects, meaning the rappings had nothing to do with spirits at all.

In the end, it may not matter. From a historical perspective, one must be amazed that two young girls from a tiny farm community caused a stir that captured the attention of millions of Americans for more than half a century. Spiritualism became a significant force that spurred science,

psychology, and theology to think in new ways. While it challenged long-held beliefs, it motivated millions to question the very nature of life and death. It also proved to be a very important solution to grief, especially after the Civil War. The movement that the sisters began grew to be much larger than just two women. Their confessions and recantations came too late to stop Spiritualism and the surge of interest that it created in the supernatural that continues to this day.

The story of the Fox sisters was merely the beginning of the Spiritualist movement. There were still many stories to tell.

THE KNOCKING DEAD: PART 2

SEX *in the* SEANCE ROOM

How the Women of Spiritualism Changed the World

TROY TAYLOR

ALTHOUGH MOST READERS CANNOT — THANKFULLY — COMPREHEND SUCH THINGS TODAY, THERE WAS A TIME IN AMERICAN HISTORY WHEN WOMEN WERE CONSIDERED SECOND-CLASS CITIZENS, OR WORSE. UNABLE TO VOTE, UNABLE TO PRACTICE MEDICINE OR LAW, UNABLE TO EASILY OBTAIN A DIVORCE, EVEN IN THE DIREST CIRCUMSTANCES, WOMEN WERE TREATED IN A FASHION THAT DID NOT EVEN APPROACH "UNEQUAL" –– IT WAS FAR WORSE THAN THAT.

IN MANY WAYS, IT WAS SPIRITUALISM THAT BEGAN TO CHANGE THOSE THINGS.

By the middle nineteenth century, men had been running things in America for so long that no one could remember life being any other way. American society was all neatly structured - men went to work; they were the breadwinners, the leaders and the decision-makers; they made and enforced all the laws. They could mistreat and abuse their wives in any way that they wanted, and many did. It was not illegal, and often not even frowned upon, for a man to beat his wife. Women were meant to remain at home, obedient and duty-bound, to tend to the household and raise the children. If a woman chose or was forced to work, it was generally in the poorest-paying occupations. With the exception of teachers, headmistresses, midwives, and a handful of writers and poets, there were few opportunities for women. If they needed employment to support themselves and family members, it was for wages that were well below what men earned, and in a job such as servant, domestic, mill worker, seamstress, or laundress. As America became more industrialized, many young women worked 16 hours a day in factories for pathetically little money and under terrible conditions. Prostitution was common in every city, large and small.

The legal rights of women were severely limited, if they existed at all. Once they married, rich or poor, women essentially became the property of their husbands. Their most important function was providing children. It was not unusual for desperately poor girls and young women who became pregnant to abandon or murder their babies. There were no social service programs, as we know them today, and there was little help offered to women and girls who were living in wretched poverty.

When a woman married, she had no property rights and if she worked, her salary went to her husband. By law, she could not withhold sex from her husband, no matter what the circumstances were. Seeking a divorce meant disgrace and forfeiting the custody of her children. Women could not serve on juries or give testimony in court. Universities, medical, and law schools barred their admission. The right to vote was still many years away.

And while this may have been the normal state of affairs in this county, not everyone was content with this restrictive social structure. Many women chafed at the inequality and the inherent unfairness of the system. They were depressed, angry, and frustrated by its constraints and inequities. Some became physically and emotionally ill. Yet by mid-century, little progress had been made to improve the status of American women.

Then, in 1848, two important and separate events occurred in Western New York that would ultimately bring about a drastic change in the social landscape of the country. In late March of that year, the Fox sisters reported spirit rappings in their Hydesville home and the Spiritualist movement was born. Across the country, interest in communicating with the dead became so popular, so quickly, that many were caught off guard. Mediums and séances seemed to emerge virtually overnight in nearly every town and city in the country. The movement attracted several million adherents in a short amount of time and became a sensation.

The other important event was the emergence of a movement supporting women's rights. Not far from Rochester, New York, where Kate and Margaret Fox moved during the summer of 1848 and took along their astonishing spirit raps, a landmark gathering occurred in the village of Seneca Falls. It was a conference about women's rights, and it had been organized by two women dubbed as "firebrands," a moniker that was either positive or negative, depending on which side of the fence you were on. Elizabeth Cady Stanton and Lucretia Mott were great leaders - or outrageous agitators, some would say. They had organized the Seneca Falls Convention to deliberate women's equality and press for "social, civil and religious rights."

Elizabeth Cady Stanton and Lucretia Mott

Stanton, a native of upstate New York and a soon-to-be Spiritualist, had heard the Fox sisters' spirit raps. Mott was a Quaker from Philadelphia. There were far fewer members of her faith in New York, but all of them were deeply committed to social causes and were considered among the "liberal religions," which also included Unitarians and Universalists. For example, in Rochester, the Quaker community numbered less than 600, but all of them were involved in the abolitionist movement and actively assisted slaves who escaped from the South on the Underground Railroad. Many Quakers also became deeply involved in both the Spiritualist movement and the cause for women's rights.

Spiritualists, by their own definition, opposed Christian orthodoxy and churches that preached centuries-old dogma. Spiritualism's emphasis was on personal responsibility and the right of the individual to find God and salvation in his or her own way. Therefore, it was not surprising that Spiritualism embraced the women's movement, as well as later reform efforts for temperance, prisons, and labor. Spiritualists represented rebellion against death and rebellion against authority. They saw the need for women to move beyond their traditional roles. In fact, many consider Spiritualism to a very important - if not the *most* important -- vehicle for the spread of women's rights in mid-nineteenth century America.

Women could not be ordained as clergy in Christian churches. In fact, many churches banned them from even publicly addressing congregations. The ban stemmed from a biblical prohibition against women "preaching in public," first stated by St. Paul in the New Testament. In contrast, within the Spiritualist movement, men and women had equal standing and, as those who most often communed with the dead, women assumed leadership roles. This caused Spiritualism and women's rights to become forever intertwined.

While most men ignored or scoffed at foolish talk about women assuming positions of power, influence, and authority through hard work or schooling, by mid-century there was an angry undercurrent that grew into the women's rights movement, stirred by strong and determined leaders like Susan B. Anthony, Elizabeth Cady Stanton, and several others.

Spiritualism's contribution to the emancipation of women was significant. The Fox sisters and their spirit rappings came along at just the right time and they tore apart the males-only mentality that was taken for granted in American society. Despite the fact that there were a number of male mediums, once the Spiritualist movement became so readily identified with women and girls, it was a perception that remained intact for generations, well into the twentieth century. For many women, Spiritualism opened a door to career opportunities that were virtually unprecedented.

The reception that women mediums received, however, was mixed at first. Primarily, the chief opposition came from religion, not science, at least in the beginning. The noted jurist Oliver Wendell Holmes called the Fox sisters the "Nemesis of the pulpit." The press was largely antagonistic toward Spiritualism and many newspapers took note of the connection between mediumship and femininity. A newspaper article in 1850 even labeled some male mediums as "addled-headed feminine men." Eventually, when studies were conducted, it was found that by the end of the nineteenth century, as many as 80-percent of mediums were women.

By the days when the Spiritualist movement began its rise, Americans had progressed quite some distance in their religious beliefs from the time when women associated with the supernatural were tried and hanged as witches. Spiritualists tried hard to distance themselves from the occult with its stereotypes of witches and evil spells and by the middle 1800s, regarded their principles as a "scientific religion." But there were still many fundamentalist preachers who attempted to convince Christians that Spiritualism was the "work of the

Devil," and some went even farther, branding mediums as the "witches" they tried so hard not to appear to be. Most Americans had moved beyond the fire and brimstone doctrines of the early nineteenth century, especially in the North, so such preaching by evangelical ministers found a limited audience. The Catholic Church decided not to take any chances with Spiritualism and simply forbade Catholics from consulting mediums or attending séances altogether.

Spiritualism had become a force to be reckoned with and was a concern to many established Christian denominations. It also posed a threat of a social and political nature. The movement was upsetting the very foundation of church and society. Spiritualism's close ties to the new women's rights crusade created a two-fold problem. Both radical movements had the potential to weaken Christian conformity while, at the same time, challenge the traditional role of women. Spiritualists were strong advocates for a women's right to vote as a means of "political empowerment."

Who exactly were the mediums, those women behind the curtain in the Spiritualist séance rooms, who traveled around the country to speak to the dead - and why had they chosen to do so?

For one thing, mediumship was a career that afforded women a degree of independence during a time when such a thing was rare. It also gave women a measure of attention and importance that few other occupations offered in the nineteenth century. Curiously, few women saw mediumship as a way of earning a large amount of money. For most male and female mediums who charged for séances, the compensation was actually a modest one. If asked, most replied that they felt a "calling" to bring communications from the spirit world. For many, that may well have been true, for few of them ever achieved wealth. Some claimed that they had not even wanted to demonstrate their abilities in public, but the spirits insisted that they do so.

The fact that some requested a fee for séances became controversial. There were many critics who lashed out that mediums who had been given a "spiritual gift" had no right to accept money. After all, they had not attended school or had any formal training. Spiritualists countered that by saying that mediums had expenses, as did everyone, and, therefore, had every right to a fee. As far as not requiring an education to conduct séances, mediums reminded critics that they provided a skill and ability that few had. Asking to be paid for providing a service that helped many people - especially the bereaved - was not unreasonable.

That raised another question from skeptics: If a medium charged a price for attending a séance, was the client certain that he or she had chosen a genuine medium? Fraud was rampant in the movement, even in the early years, and there was a question as to how many people had paid for bogus séances. For legitimate mediums, this was a serious concern, and they understood the difficult task of building a reputation for honesty if they wanted people to pay, especially when there was competition from many charlatans.

Some did not request to be paid at all. Nettie Colburn Maynard, who was the favorite medium of Abraham and Mary Lincoln and helped them cope with the death of their son, Willie, never charged for sittings. She had to earn a living working in a government office by day, while conducting séances at the White House and private homes in the city in the evening.

Nettie Colburn Maynard, the favorite spirit medium of President and Mrs. Lincoln

The Fox sisters, on the other hand, nearly always asked for a fee when they held séances or put on public demonstrations. Kate and Margaret both died in poverty, though, exploited by their older sister, Leah, who enjoyed a comfortable living as a manager and a medium.

A medium earned between $400 and $600 each year, a modest sum even in the economy of the mid-nineteenth century. However, most of the women who became professional mediums were from poor backgrounds and it's doubtful that they could have earned more than that in another line

Female mediums were often dismissed as "witches" or "vulgar women" but few could dispute the fact that they were adept at their craft.

of work. No one has a precise figure as to how many female mediums there were in America at that time, but to say that there were several thousand would not be an exaggeration.

Spiritualist publications, like *Banner of Light* and others, advertised mediums and the fees that they charged. A private sitting in a medium's home, for instance, was usually $1. If the medium came to the client's home, they usually charged up to $5. The same periodicals often printed letters from mediums who complained about poor compensation and the difficulty of the work. For the most part, though, they maintained their commitment to Spiritualism.

Most mediums felt positive about what they were doing, but it was not an opinion shared by everyone. Skeptics and critics found nothing commendable about the so-called "feminine" personality required to be a medium. These women "represented above all else the corruption of femininity," because they were daring to speak up, speak out, and venture outside of the home. Mediums who earned their own way didn't require a man to take care of them, a fact that most men of the era despised.

Even so, both friends and foes of Spiritualism agreed on the fact that women were best-suited to be mediums. Men decided that a woman's enhanced sensitivity and spirituality, as well as her intuitive nature, passivity, and tendency toward "nervousness" were all qualities that a good medium required. A woman was believed to be more virtuous than men, and more willing to sacrifice herself for others, even if it meant suffering, bearing pain, or foregoing her own happiness. In fact, these were the same qualities that women were thought to employ as a wife and mother. Stereotypical masculine traits such as strength, willpower, and logical thinking were supposedly not seen in mediums, at least according to the Victorian view. A man with an aggressive, intense, or forceful personality -- all considered authentic male characteristics -- would not make a good medium, they said.

If you wanted a real expert and "scientific" opinion about these qualities, phrenologists who had studied such matters supported the idea that females were better suited as mediums than men. Phrenology was the study of the shape and size of the cranium as a supposed indication of character and mental abilities. It was later discredited as a science but was taken seriously at the time. Experts stated that the shape and size of a woman's cranium indicated the necessary character and mental faculties for this type of work.

Although Victorian era generalizations and sensibilities may seem silly to modern readers, they were accepted by nearly all women and men in their day. But women mediums applied a positive spin to the labels that were assigned to them by critics. Yes, many women acknowledged, they were willing to

"sacrifice for the spiritual benefit of others," but female mediums saw their "sacrifice" as an indication of how important their work really was.

Women who were Spiritualist mediums not only attained a certain distinction, but they also achieved entry into the male-controlled world of the time. Where else in nineteenth-century America could a young woman, like Nettie Colburn Maynard or Kate Fox, dare to offer advice to the President of the United States? Was there any other place but a séance where a woman could express her opinions to men, including some of the most important figures in the country in the fields of business, law, literature, science and politics -- all of which were closed to women? These men listened to what they were told, a rarity in an era when a woman's voice was largely ignored. Female mediums suddenly had the freedom to say things in public that would be unthinkable in any other situation. Spiritualist séances and lectures were among the very few venues where women were even given a chance to speak in public.

Even better, a medium could claim immunity from anything disagreeable that she might say, stating that she'd merely been given the message to speak by the spirits while in a trance. Therefore, if a male sitter was not pleased, it was not the medium's fault. She was a passive conduit who merely repeated what the spirits passed along to her. A man couldn't blame the medium.

She did not control the spirits - the spirits controlled her.

DEFYING THE TRADITIONS OF THE DAY

While many women mediums conducted séances in private homes or settings, some women broke another social barrier by appearing in public before audiences who paid to see her. These mediums - usually called "trance speakers" - often became very well known. During the Victorian era, women were seriously discouraged from public speaking because it was thought to be inappropriate. But trance speakers defied that prohibition. They earned a slightly better income than those who gave private séances, and trance speaking fascinated audiences. Typically, there was a $1 fee per person. However, when mediums traveled, they were responsible for their own expenses, which diminished their income. Traveling was not easy or comfortable

during the nineteenth century, especially for women, so those who toured as trance speakers required stamina, in addition to the energy they needed for their demonstrations. It was not a glamorous life. Audience size and reaction varied from town to town. Meanwhile, wherever female mediums went, fundamentalist ministers attacked them for doing the work of the Devil, while secular critics branded the whole business as fraud.

Some trance speakers became very well-known. These women were known largely for offering inspiration lectures under control of the spirits. The subjects they spoke were often chosen at random by scientists and each were addressed with remarkable eloquence. It was assumed that trance speakers would not have known anything of the subjects they spoke about without help from the spirits.

Some of these traveling speakers were lucky when it came to money. For instance, trance medium Samantha Mettler used her income to help support her family when her husband's business fell into bankruptcy. But others were badly exploited, often taken advantage of by fathers and husbands. When that occurred, there was little if anything that could be done about it.

Occasionally, female mediums earned the attention of a wealthy patron who provided her with a respectable income. During the nineteenth century, there were several successful and affluent men who paid mediums exclusively to hold their own private séances. Cornelius J. Vanderbilt, Henry Seybert, David Underhill, and Horace Day were among the

rich and powerful who employed their own mediums this way. Even a woman who was a fraud might find herself lucky enough to cash in. In New York during the 1880s, such a thing happened for an infamous and spurious medium named Madame Debar, when a wealthy attorney provided her with an elegant home, the *New York Times* reported.

Another understandable lure for women who became mediums was for the attention they received. Whether it was criticism or praise, it was a way to gain notoriety that no other occupation provided. For a young woman who'd had an unhappy or lonely childhood, as many did, mediumship became an escape, and at the same time, it attracted public notice. For some, any attention was better than none.

There were many "lady trance mediums" who achieved fame in the nineteenth century. And none of them could have been as "frail and passive" as their male critics claimed. If we consider the thousands of miles they traveled on poorly paved and rutted roads, in every kind of weather, by horse, wagon, carriage, coach, boat, and train, then they must have been truly hale and hearty adventurers, equal to any man of the day.

"MRS. SATAN" FOR AMERICA

There were few things that captured the attention of the nineteenth century public like Spiritualism did. Spiritualism moved women into the spotlight of public attention in a way that nothing had ever been able to do before and perhaps for this reason, as the movement changed and adapted through the decades, it became more galvanizing, more controversial - and definitely more fascinated with sex.

In hindsight, such a development was completely understandable. There were a number of things that were largely seen as taboo during this era - communication with spirits, women's rights, and sex. We have already demonstrated the links between the emancipation of women and the Spiritualist movement, and it's easy to understand why more openness about sex soon followed.

Needless to say, this led to controversy, both in the bedroom and out of it. There were plenty of marital problems in the nineteenth century and that ha snot changed much over the years. However, because a divorced woman was often stigmatized, and her options to leave her husband were few, there was less divorce than there is now. But there were perhaps even more unhappy marriages, as well as outrageous amounts of wife and child abuse, alcoholic husbands, and men who simply deserted their families. Many women who became mediums understood these problems, because many - although not all -- came from similar backgrounds.

In cases where mediums learned that their female clients had serious marital problems, or were in danger because of physical or sexual abuse, and with no laws to protect them, the *spirits* often advised that "wives divorce their husbands." Outraged critics charged that female mediums were encouraging "immoral behavior," but, of course, the mediums could always say the spirits were to blame. For Spiritualists, divorce seemed a reasonable response to misery and abuse. For the more conservative, divorce for a woman was not considered an option, and Spiritualist advice to the contrary posed a grave threat to family stability. The critics stated that mediums were nonconformists, and symbolized defiance of nineteenth century values.

There's no question, there were a threat to "nineteenth century values" - and for good reason. Women were second-class citizens for most of society. Within the Spiritualist community, though, women were leaders and spokespersons, which they could not be in everyday life. There were many double standards for women at the time, especially when it came to sex. Female trance speakers often traveled alone, and there's no question that some of them found themselves in circumstances that permitted promiscuity. Even during séances, some women mediums had the opportunity to do things under the cover of darkness that they never would have done in polite society. Séances were held that involved scantily clad "apparitions" and mediums were quick to disrobe to prove that they had hidden no ghostly props under their clothing. Spirit summonings were conducted in lingerie, filmy shifts, and, in some cases, nothing at all.

Critics were outraged. This was activity that defied the rigid Victorian standards. The strict morality of the nineteenth century did not encourage sexual relations -- except for procreation by married couples. Public discussions of sex were taboo and, most of the time, the subject was avoided in private, too. Of course, many mediums and Spiritualists ignored propriety, just as many non-Spiritualists did, but this issue provided enemies of Spiritualism and women's rights with another line of attack.

Conservatives particularly accused Spiritualists of supporting "free love," which, in those days, meant "promiscuity and infidelity." Because of this, Spiritualists posed a threat to the "sacred institution" of marriage and shocked religious opponents. Actually, most Spiritualists were not in favor of free love, but the two became connected in the public mind. This connection was formed because it was said that many women Spiritualists criticized "marriage as the root of women's oppression," wrote Ann Braude.

Spiritualists did not oppose marriage. What they vehemently criticized was the unfairness of marriage and the laws that deprived women of equal rights, kept them subservient, and often amounted to their subjugation by men. Further, Spiritualists argued, women were frequently forced to marry because of a lack of economic opportunities, and then have children, whether they wanted to or not. The answer was not to abolish marriage, but to improve the laws that governed it. All of this is largely a general rule today, but it was

Victoria Woodhull, the first women to campaign to be President of the United States, was referred to as "Mrs. Satan" by critics who despised her.

a groundbreaking attitude in the nineteenth century and was harshly criticized by the majority of society.

As the years passed, Spiritualism became more steeped in controversy when it came to women's rights, as is apparent in the story of the first woman -- a spirit medium -- who ran for President.

In 1872, a woman named Victoria Woodhull became the first woman to try and become President of the United States. She had an uphill battle ahead of her. As a woman, she wasn't even allowed to vote. If elected,

she would have been too young at the age of 34 to serve, but it didn't matter because she only received a handful of votes. Even her running mate, Frederick Douglass, voted for President Ulysses S. Grant. On Election Day, she was in jail for slandering the most famous minister in the country.

When Hillary Clinton was nominated as the Democratic Party's choice for the presidency in 2016, Victoria Woodhull, a largely forgotten novelty in the historical record, was suddenly in the spotlight for the first time in more than a century and a half. She began to be lauded for her trailblazing advocacy of woman's rights - including the movement for "free love" and divorce - and her work in the suffrage movement of the day. But what most people neglect to mention is that Victoria Woodhull didn't achieve her greatest notoriety as a presidential nominee, but rather as a Spiritualist medium who started the first female brokerage firm on Wall Street by charging some of the nation's wealthiest men to contact the dead.

When someone once asked shipping magnate, financier, and railroad tycoon Cornelius Vanderbilt for financial advice, he replied, "Do as

I do, consult the spirits!" His conduit between this world and the next was Victoria Woodhull.

Born Victoria Clafflin in Homer, Ohio, in September 1838, her childhood was a nightmare. Her mother was an eccentric who had "memorized the Bible backward and forward." Her father was a con artist who abused his family and was once described by a neighbor as a "one-eyed, one-man crime spree." He fled town after allegedly burning down his own mill for the insurance money and stealing petty cash from the post office. Locals took up a collection so that his family could follow him. Victoria was the seventh of ten children, four of whom did not live to adulthood. She had only a few years of formal education before being put to work in her father's traveling medicine show. She and her younger sister, Tennessee, gave séances, performed as fortune tellers, and sold fake elixirs to the gullible.

At age 15, she was married for the first time to a drunken, philandering physician named Canning Woodhull. They had two children together but divorced in 1864. She later married two more times.

In 1868, Victoria and Tennessee moved to New York City, where

Victoria became the personal spirit medium of tycoon Cornelius Vanderbilt and managed to build a fortune of her own.

business and industry were growing rapidly in the years after the Civil War. Millionaires were being made in the shipping, construction, and railroad businesses, and through a series of fortunate coincidences that put the sisters in the right place at the right time, they met tycoon Cornelius Vanderbilt. He was the richest man in America, had an eye for beautiful women, and was obsessed with contacting his late mother. Victoria soon became his personal spirit medium.

Within two years, using the stock advice that was gleaned from the "spirits" during her séances with Vanderbilt, Victoria and Tennessee became known as the "lady brokers." Vanderbilt helped them to establish a stock brokerage office, the first of its kind for women of that era. The sisters did very well financially and realized a sizable profit.

With some of their earnings, they established a weekly newspaper that was designed to cast attention on topics that were of interest to feminists of the time, such as equal rights and suffrage. In 1871, Victoria and her political positions had become so well-known that she appeared before the House Judiciary Committee to speak on behalf of women's rights. In doing so, she became the first women to ever testify before a congressional committee.

But her stance on women's rights was not what earned her the nickname of "Mrs. Satan." That came about because of her support of another controversial topic of the time: free love. She believed in the right of a woman "to love who I want for as long as I want," then to divorce. Under the law, she said, marriage for women was slavery. By the age of 31, she was a millionaire, but when she walked into Delmonico's restaurant without a male escort, she was refused a seat. She

tried to vote in 1871, claiming that the 14th Amendment guaranteed women that right. As she had told the congressional committee, "We don't need the right to vote, we have it."

But it was in 1872, that Victoria Woodhull truly earned her place in American history when she ran for president. It was a daring move that caught the attention of the press, politicians, and the public. It was the first time that a woman - and a Spiritualist - sought the highest office in the land. She won the nomination of the Equal Rights Party. The former slave and abolitionist Frederick Douglass was named as her running mate, but if he knew it, he never acknowledged the nomination and campaigned for President Grant.

Even though Victoria could have never been elected, none of that mattered. Her goal was to call attention to women's rights issues - and to herself. Few regarded Victoria's candidacy seriously; but the press was more than happy to write about her efforts because it sold newspapers. During her run, she did gain support from a few women's rights groups and from some Spiritualists, but her radical position toward free love alienated most of those who would have helped her.

Conservative newspapers and religious organizations began accusing every one of America's four million or more Spiritualists of supporting free love and while it was a false charge, it inflamed passions.

Things turned ugly during her campaign. Reverend Henry Ward Beecher, brother of *Uncle Tom's Cabin* author Harriet Beecher Stowe, had attacked Victoria's notion of free love from his Brooklyn pulpit. Shortly before the election, Victoria's newspaper printed a story that revealed that Beecher was having an adulterous affair with a parishioner, Mrs. Elizabeth Tilton. The result of the allegations was a full-blown scandal and an embarrassing trial for Beecher on adultery charges.

The newspaper story may have been accurate, but under a federal law against mailing "obscene" material, Victoria was arrested and jailed, where she spent Election Day. By the way, the winner of the 1872 election was Ulysses S. Grant, who went on to a second term in office.

In the wake of the scandal, her arrest, and the election, Victoria was called a "vile jailbird" by Harriet Beecher Stowe and an "impudent witch." Others called her much worse. She was later cleared at trial, but the events ruined her health, her finances, and her reputation. In 1877, she moved to England, where she married a banker, still supported liberal causes, and lived comfortably until her death in 1927.

She seemed destined for historical oblivion. The Spiritualists wanted nothing to do with her because they believed that she had used the movement to simply further her radical women's rights agenda. Following the Civil War, when so many people were seeking mediums to contact their loved ones, Victoria Woodhull had soured the movement's reputation. The bereaved were more concerned with speaking with their loved ones than with listening to speeches about social injustice.

Victoria's radical position on free love had caused rifts within the women's rights movement, as well. Even bold feminist leaders like Susan B. Anthony, who had once welcomed Victoria, later distanced herself. When Anthony and Elizabeth Cady Stanton wrote a six-volume history of the suffrage movement, Victoria's contributions were reduced to one brief mention.

She would likely have been forgotten altogether - along with her presidential candidacy -- if not for another, far different woman who made history in 2016.

SEX IN THE SEANCE ROOM

Spiritualism changed after the Civil War, which brought staggering death tolls -- and a staggering number of people who wanted to reach those who had died in the conflict. By the 1870s, mediums had become so prevalent that they were forced to step up their showmanship to retain their audiences. Many spectacular displays were reported that seemed to have more to do with the theatrical than the spiritual. Flying objects, birds, musical instruments, glowing spirit hands, table tipping, and spirit materializations all became séance staples. As the dazzling and dramatic became such an important part of séances, Spiritualism's credibility became increasingly challenged. The press and the clergy were as hostile as ever and some scientists had joined the skeptics in their efforts to debunk the entire movement. With the exposure of many physical mediums as frauds, and their array of effects shown to be tricks, Spiritualism was barraged with criticism.

And then when mediums added sex to the mix, things got even wilder.

Spiritualism was born in an era of scientific and literary achievement, but many people turned to a belief in the spirit world as an antidote to the scholarly agnosticism that could be found in the daily newspapers and on the lips of scientists and writers. It was also an escape from the restrictions of society. Many faithful Spiritualists used the séance chamber as a way to express their need to explore new things, to seek out ideas that were seen as beyond the norm, and also as a way to express sexual needs, wants, and desires. When interacting with the spirits was not titillating enough, mixing in a little eroticism guaranteed that the evening would become more exciting. For this reason, we can never underestimate the role that sex played in the Spiritualist movement.

By the later years of the nineteenth century, Spiritualism had become engorged with sex - if you take my meaning -- although this was largely unknown by the public. Unless someone was an actual participant in a séance, or part of an experiment to test the skills of a medium, they were unlikely to read about what was taking place in the séance room. Sex was simply not something that was discussed in public, let alone in newspapers and scientific journals.

In reading the reports of the era, though, it's clear that there existed a strong and scientific connection between mediumship and sex, although it went carefully unmentioned. Dr. W.J. Crawford, a lecturer in mechanical engineering at the Municipal Technical Institute at Belfast, Ireland, carried out a long series of experiments that he devised for the purpose of finding out what part of medium Kathleen Goligher's body produced the mysterious psychic substance known as ectoplasm. The experiments were based on his findings that a type of powder would stick to the ectoplasm and that by placing the powder on the medium's shoes and around her legs, the track of the ectoplasm could be revealed. Careful as he was in his choice of words -- speaking about the "top of the stockings" and "inside the legs of the knickers to the joint of the legs" or the ectoplasm returning "by way of the trunk" -- it was clear that he was referring to the ectoplasm coming from the medium's vagina, even if he didn't come right out and say it.

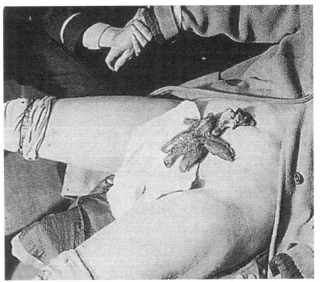

Ectoplasm appears from a medium's vagina in this photograph taken in the 1920s.

See the next article by Amanda Woomer for more on this!

For plainer language, there is Baron Schrenck-Notzing's account of the mediumship of Willie Schneider: "With the increase of phenomena, the bodily movements became stronger, the clonic shakings more powerful, cramp-like, the pulse flew up and the respiration grew labored. Perspiration stood on the forehead of the medium. The whole process is very much like a birth process. Biologically, the erotic activity is unmistakable."

Another report about Schneider came from Dr. W. Osborne: "Finally, I could not fail to observe that all of the phenomena produced by an effort on

The medium who used the stage name "Eva C." producing ectoplasm on camera in 1912. She often performed her seances in the nude.

the part of the medium, who perspires very strongly during the demonstration, point to happenings which hang together with the sexual sphere of the medium. It is difficult to make accurate observations in this respect, but the whole corporeal attitude of the medium during and before the phenomenon, the cramp-like increase of the totality of body energies, the rhythm of his movements, his great general excitement which strives to reach a high point after the achievement of which the phenomena begin and the medium is visibly exhausted and satisfied, speak for the idea that these things somehow hang together with his sex."

General Joseph Peter of Munich also wrote about Willie Schneider: "The medium, as the phenomena was about to happen, was often in fear and excitement. Willie pressed himself trembling to me and groaned in anxiety. From time to time, however, it seemed he was possessed by erotic feelings; he stroked the hands of his controls with his cheek and began to bite me on the arm. 'Mina' --his female controlling spirit -- would only desist after very emphatic requests."

There was a lot of heavy breathing going on in the séance room.

Many mediums were known to have experienced sexual thrills while "entranced." Although the word "orgasm" was not mentioned by researchers, they did use "voluptuous," "sensual," and "climax," if they were feeling unusually daring. It was rumored that the distinguished scientist Sir William Crookes was infatuated with his young medium, Florence Cook, who was caught flitting around the séance room in her underthings by Sir George Sitwell. Mediums like Victoria Woodhull advocated "free love" and were not above using their charms to fascinate clients like Cornelius Vanderbilt. And the list went on.

There is no question that the séance room could be a fevered place. Mediums were often strip-searched and tied to chairs. Fraudulent ones stripped off their clothes to impersonate spirits. Spirits fondled legs, patted thighs, and kissed sitters in the dark. In comparison to the everyday segregation of sexes at that time, séances could be a thrilling experience.

Famous Italian medium Eusapia Palladino, was one of the most sexual Spiritualists of the early 1900s. She claimed that after excessive mediumistic practice, she would bleed more freely during menstruation. Her trance states were also very peculiar, especially to some of the strait-laced observers of the time. Enrico Morselli wrote: "The passing into a more advanced state of trance is truly indicated by sighs, yawns, sobs, of alternating redness and pallor of the face, perspiration on the forehead, light transparency of the palms of the hands, the alteration of voice and the quick changes of facial expression.

Eusapia then progresses through a diversity of emotional states and now she is prey to a species of concentrated rage which she expresses with quick movements, with imperious commands, with sarcastic phrases directed at her critics, with smiles and loud laughter which is something diabolical. Then she passes into a state of decided voluptuous ecstasy, throwing about both her arms, squeezing us with her tensed thighs and trembling feet, resting her head and abandoning her whole body on my or Barzini's shoulders while we fearlessly resist this innocent attack against our masculine emotions."

Simply put, sex could not be disassociated from Spiritualism because mediums were human beings. They either had a normal, if somewhat impaired, sex life, or they had none, in which case something abnormal was likely to happen. If the energies bound up within the body cannot be released in a physical way, then it would certainly be expended in some other manner. In mediumship, sexual energies may have furnished fuel for the many physical, and perhaps mental, manifestations that occurred during séances.

In other cases, the things that happened were just plain weird -- and

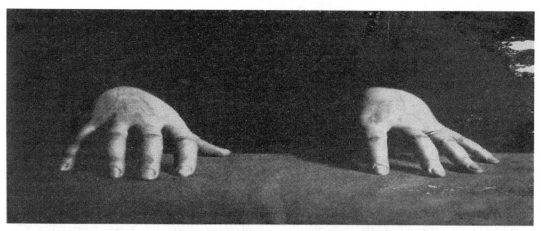

EUSAPIA PALLADINO BECAME ALMOST SINGLE-HANDEDLY RESPONSIBLE FOR RESTORING THE PRESTIGE OF PHYSICAL MEDIUMSHIP AND WENT ON TO BECOME PERHAPS THE MOST FAMOUS — AND CONTROVERSIAL -- MEDIUM OF THE PERIOD.

far too shocking for some of the strait-laced investigators of the time.

SEX AND THE SPIRIT MEDIUM

Toward the end of the nineteenth century, the rise of Spiritualist organizations caused a relative decline in the sort of mediumship practiced by some of the early members of the movement, who were often exposed as frauds. New, organized groups began taking steps to examine the claims of their own members and they did so with such thoroughness that mediums - both good and bad -- began to act with caution. Exuberant exhibitions with trumpets, rope tricks, and whirling ghosts began to quietly fade away.

This is not to say that physical mediumship began to disappear from the scene, but in the 1880s, the emphasis began to shift away from tipping tables and tooting horns to a more serious attempt to examine those proofs of spirit existence in the form of messages and information. Commercial mediumship suffered for a time, but people began to speak about the legitimacy of the movement for the first time in -- well, ever.

And then along came Eusapia Palladino. This Italian peasant woman became almost single-handedly responsible for restoring the prestige of physical mediumship and went on to become perhaps the most famous - and controversial -- medium of the period.

If respected spirit mediums had truly begun to acquire an air of respectability, it only took Eusapia Palladino to upset the wagon and get critics in an uproar again.

Eusapia was born near Bari in southern Italy in 1854. Her mother died shortly after she was born and her father was murdered in 1866, leaving Eusapia an orphan at the age of 12. Even then, it was later reported, she had already experienced many strange and supernatural events, such as rapping sounds on the furniture, eerie whispers, and unseen hands that would rip the blankets from her bed at night.

Friends and relatives sent Eusapia to Naples, where it was hoped that she would find a position as a nursemaid. Things did not go well. The family that hired her was disturbed by the fact that eerie events occurred around the young woman and were bothered by the fact that Eusapia refused to conform to life in the city. She had a stubborn streak that ran through her character, which often showed itself in her refusal to take a bath, comb her hair, or learn to read. She was soon dismissed from her position.

She took shelter with some family friends who dabbled in Spiritualism. Eusapia attended a séance one night and almost as soon as she sat down at the table, it tilted and then rose completely into the air. She began to act as a medium to reportedly avoid being sent to a convent, although she claimed that she was afraid of her powers and avoided using them. The family with whom she was living asked Eusapia to stay on with them, and continue holding séances, but with her typical stubbornness, she moved out and began to work as a laundress. She later married a merchant named

Raphael Delgaiz and worked in his shop for a time before starting to offer séances on a professional basis.

In 1872, a wealthy and influential Spiritualist couple named Damiani sought Eusapia out. They had heard good things about the séances that she had been conducting and wanted to introduce her into society. Unfortunately, the coarse and rude young woman was no more interested in education and social polish than she had been years before and her introduction was a disaster. The Damianis' efforts to develop and study Eusapia's powers proved thankless, and she lapsed back into a life of ordinary mediumship, virtually unknown outside of a small circle in Naples.

In this way, Eusapia would have lived out her entire life, if she had not come to the attention of Ercole Chiaia, a doctor and dabbler in the occult, who sought her out in 1886. Acting almost like a manager, Chiaia took upon himself to publish an open letter to the famed Italian psychiatrist and criminologist Cesare Lombroso. In the letter, which he wrote as if describing a patient, Chiaia gave a summary of Eusapia's mediumistic abilities and urgently requested Lombroso's help in determining whether she possessed some sort of new physical force. The letter turned out to be a stroke of genius for Eusapia's career. Even though Lombroso ignored the letter at first, the interest surrounding it gave her fortunes an immediate boost because it finally put her into the public spotlight.

The letter described happenings that were typical of her career so far. Most of the incidents in the letter were common to séances performed by physical mediums, but others were much rarer -- and harder to explain. What, for example, was to be made of the phantom feet and limbs that appeared, were studied, and could not be debunked? Nearly the entire history of Palladino's next 30 years was devoted to accounts of the committees and investigators who sought to answer these, and other, mysteries about her.

It took two years, but Cesare Lombroso turned out to be the first major researcher to seek Eusapia out. He came to Naples in 1890 and arranged to hold several private séances with his at his hotel. Most of these initial sessions feel short of what Eusapia was usually capable of, with one exception. At the close of one séance, the lights had been turned up

Photographs taken during a séance with Eusapia show a table seemingly levitation off the floor. Such events were said to be common during her sessions.

and the observers were discussing their impressions while Eusapia was still tied to a chair, about 18 inches in front of the curtain that formed her spirit cabinet. Suddenly, sounds were heard from the alcove behind her, the curtain began to swing and billow forward, and then a small table emerged from behind it and began to slide across the floor towards the medium. Lombroso and his associates hurried into the cabinet, convinced that a confederate must be hiding inside, but it was empty, save for a few musical instruments. The observers were stumped, and Lombroso dismissed any previous doubts that he had about Eusapia's abilities. He had no explanation for what he had seen.

Lombroso published a report of his findings, and it was greeted with both shock and surprise. Lombroso had an excellent reputation as a psychiatrist who often helped the police with difficult cases - sort of a nineteenth century "profiler" - and if

In another photo from one of Eusapia's seances, a table is again seen levitating off the floor. If it was trickery, no one was able to catch her at it - this time, at least.

he could be so readily convinced of Palladino's paranormal talents, then there must be something truly amazing about this woman. Other investigators began contacting the medium and in October 1892, Eusapia was asked to sit for a scientific committee in Milan. Among its five members were Lombroso himself and Professor Charles Richet, a noted student of psychic phenomena and a man who would go on to win the Nobel Prize for physiology and medicine in

1913. His interest in the paranormal was ignited by Eusapia and he went on to publish several books about psychic phenomena and investigate other mediums during his career.

The séances that were held for the Milan committee were the first of which there were relatively reliable records concerning the manifestations of Palladino. They are also the first to not only make note of unexplained occurrences, but also of something else that would shadow the career of the medium: Eusapia cheated.

There was no question whatsoever, even among her most ardent supporters, that she took advantage of every lapse in attention or muscular relaxation on the part of those who were supposed to "control" her movements, so that she could produce touches, raps, or movements of objects by erroneous methods. Sometimes her tricks were clumsy and obvious and at other times, subtle and clever, but it could not be denied that she cheated. It seemed to make no difference to her that she might be exposed in these activities -- as she repeatedly was. Given the slightest opportunity, Eusapia cheated.

One of her most common ruses was to convince the two people assigned to hold her arms that each had continued to keep contact with a separate limb, when actually, one of them had transferred his hand to her other arm. This was possible because Eusapia constantly moved about while in her trances, thrashing restlessly back and forth. As she rocked back and forth, tossed her head, and waved her arms about, it took great skill on the part of the handlers to be sure they were not both controlling the same hand. This was especially true as the handlers were usually allowed only to follow the medium's hands by touch but not to restrain her movements in any way. Because of all the excitement, it was also nearly impossible to decide if Eusapia's hands were where they were supposed to be.

But yet, Eusapia was a complete enigma -- she cheated, but not always. The eyewitness reports made it clear that she would cheat whenever she could, but there were also manifestations that occurred that could not be explained. During the sessions, which were held by a dim red light, members could see and feel what were apparently several spectral hands that groped outward from behind the cabinet curtain while the medium remained plainly visible in front of them. Chairs moved, tables lifted, objects took flight. All of this

occurred while Palladino was under close observation. Photographs were taken of her manifestations in action. The lights were on, there were no confederates in the room, no one imagined anything -- but paranormal events occurred. There was no explanation for them. Even given the fact that Eusapia was not above faking certain effects, was it possible for anyone -- let alone a semiliterate peasant woman with no knowledge of applied mechanics -- to bring about such happenings through trickery? That is the exasperating problem that haunted the scientific minds of the time and still haunts us about Eusapia Palladino today.

Eusapia continued to baffle scientists and investigators. She performed for Russian zoologist N.P. Wagner in Naples in January 1893 and then did so again later in Rome. She sat for Polish psychologist Julian Ochorowicz in Warsaw at the end of the year and at the beginning of 1894. During every session, the results were mixed. Some of the effects that occurred were plainly the result of cheating. Some of them could have been produced by cheating, although witnesses were prepared to state that no cheating had taken place. And some of the effects were judged to be

Eusapia with Professor Henry Sidgwick in England. Her seances there did not go as planned.

inexplicable in terms of any of the methods of deception that Eusapia had so far been known to use -- and possibly inexplicable in any way whatsoever.

A more revealing series of séances was held in 1894 at the home of Professor Charles Richet in France. Almost every member of this group of sitters was major name in the fledgling field of psychical research. In addition to Richet himself, Dr. Julian Ochorowicz was present, along with the German researcher Baron von Schrenck-Notzing. There were

also four highly influential English investigators on hand -- Sir Oliver Lodge, Professor and Mrs. Henry Sidgwick, and Frederick William Henry Myers, all of whom had founded the Society for Psychical Research in England in 1882.

The entire group was very aware of the medium's tendency to cheat and the need for suspicious watchfulness. In spite of this, they observed the cabinet curtain billowing when there was no breeze, they experienced repeated "spirit touches" at times when all were certain that Eusapia could not have been responsible and saw and heard objects being moved around the séance chamber. One of these items was a large piece of fruit -- a melon that weighed more than 15 pounds. It somehow moved from a chair behind the medium to the top of the séance table. Even if Eusapia had managed to get a hand free on this occasion, it's difficult to guess how she could have grasped an object as smooth as a melon, somehow moved it from a chair behind her to a table and managed to place it on a table before the eyes of a group of trained observers. It seems impossible and because of this, alternate theories emerged to explain the incident. Some suggested that the observers had simply hallucinated the "magic melon." Others claimed that one or more of the committee members had been in league with the medium, which seems even more unlikely given the reputations of those present.

So, how did this bizarre event occur? No one knew then and no one knows now. It was after this incident that investigators came to realize that there was a need for the more extensive use of recording devices and photographs during investigations. That way, the control of the medium and the occurrence of the phenomena would not be subject to errors in human perception. Unfortunately, even after this important series of séances, such improved methods of investigation were not used with Palladino until a later period, and even then, were not as thoroughly applied as they should have been.

After the sittings in France, the next important sessions with Eusapia took place in England and were generally regarded as a disaster. Of the four English participants in the investigations of Professor Richet, only Sir Oliver Lodge had found himself completely satisfied that Eusapia's phenomena were in part paranormal. The others, Myers and the Sidgwicks, wanted further trials before they could reach firm opinions. They invited Palladino to sit for them at Myers's home in Cambridge, where she went in the late summer of 1895.

Unfortunately, no detailed record of the Cambridge séances was ever published by the SPR and so we have no way of knowing what led to the conclusions reached by those involved. We only know that in October 1895, Professor Sidgwick announced at the society's general meeting that nothing had been witnessed at Cambridge that could not be dismissed as trickery. He then went on to withdraw what limited support that he had for Palladino, based on the French sittings, and to state that he had come to believe that all her manifestations were fraudulent. Myers joined Sidgwick in rejecting the Cambridge séances, although he did choose to reserve judgment on what he had seen in France, which he claimed was more impressive.

No one knows for sure what occurred in Cambridge that summer, but it was clear there were things about Palladino that would have likely offended the Sidgwicks and their friends, regardless of the quality of her mediumship. In fact, had it not been for her inexplicable abilities, it is highly unlikely that these cultivated English people would have ever associated with a person like Eusapia. Regardless of her reputation as a medium, she did not fit into the mold of other important mediums at the time. She had none of the social graces or charm so many mediums possessed and certainly none of the sober, upright character of the upper crust SPR members and their friends. Instead, she was almost everything that her Cambridge hosts were not: poorly educated, coarse, emotional, loud, and quite uninhibited about her interest in the opposite sex.

Eusapia Palladino was crude and the complete opposite of the repressed Victorians who had invited her to England. She tended to wake from her trances hot, sweaty, and sexually aroused. On many occasions, she tried climbing onto the laps of male sitters at her séances. She was not shy in making in clear that she was looking for intercourse, or that she wanted it immediately. She was not a beautiful woman but thanks to her voluptuousness and obvious desire, she had no shortage of men who were happy to volunteer -- all for the good of the spirit world, of course.

Needless to say, Eusapia's overtly sexual behavior was considered quite unacceptable in Victorian England. The Cambridge investigators tried to make Eusapia as comfortable as possible, however, but only under their own terms. They wanted her to be in a receptive state for her séances, but there was a limit to their generosity. Professor Myers' wife took her shopping, allowed Eusapia to cook Italian meals in her kitchen, and listened to her incessant chatter, even though Mrs. Myers spoke only a few words of Italian and had no idea what Eusapia was talking about. The Myers's young son, Leo, was recruited to play croquet with her on the lawn, but the boy complained that she cheated during every game.

Eusapia was unhappy during her stay in England. She hated the climate in Cambridge, the cool summer weather, the polite conversation, and cultured people. She fell into an ill-tempered sulk that carried over into the sittings. She became indifferent about the entire situation, refused to be tied in place, sometimes wouldn't allow her feet to be held, and performed poorly. Because of this, little happened. Tables tipped a time or two, but that was about all. It's not surprising that Sidgwick and Myers had enough of the troublesome medium and withdrew their support of her after that summer.

A denunciation by the SPR should have damaged Palladino's career but as it turned out, her work was far from over. She left England and returned to Italy, where she had always felt most comfortable. She presided over numerous séances in private homes and the sitters were apparently satisfied, for she continued to be in great demand. It was not until November 1898 that Eusapia consented to be examined by another scientific committee. This time the investigation was held in Paris and the organizer was Camille Flammarion, an eminent astronomer and a student of the paranormal. One of his chief assistants was Professor Richet.

The Paris séances produced several manifestations that were familiar --- and some that were decidedly strange. During one session, Eusapia was seated at one end of a table, and controlled in the usual way, when the sitters were stunned by the sight of a series of semi-transparent female half-figures that seemed to glide out of her body and down the length of the table.

Richet apparently felt the Paris séances were so interesting that they ought to be extended, and when the sittings sponsored by Flammarion had ended --- and Flammarion himself had declared that he was satisfied that trickery could not account for what had occurred --- Eusapia consented to continue the sittings. Richet quickly organized a new series of séances and invited Frederick Myers to attend as a private individual and not as a representative of the SPR. According to their individual accounts, these further sittings were truly remarkable. But as with the Cambridge séances, it is unfortunate --- and more than a little mystifying -- that no official records exist to tell us why they were so exciting.

Whatever occurred, it led the formerly skeptical and hostile Myers to declare at the general meetings of the SPR for December 1899 that he was now convinced of Palladino's gifts. He had just witnessed, he told the group, phenomena "far more striking" than the séances that he had attended with Eusapia in 1894. However, neither Myers not Richet ever published any notes on these sittings, though in the case of Myers, the continuing negative attitude of his friends in the SPR was likely responsible for this.

The only surviving account comes to us from the unofficial notes of Professor T. Flournoy of the Faculty of Sciences at the University of Geneva, who was also present at the séances. Flournoy was an experienced observer of the Spiritualist movement but does not go into enough detail about what he saw to permit any sort of strict analysis. Regardless, there is no reason to doubt his overall description of the conditions of the séances. It's interesting to note that this time Eusapia not only agreed to produce her phenomena in a light that, while dim, was more than sufficient for her movements to be seen by the sitters, but she also allowed her wrists and legs to be firmly held rather than just followed about.

Under these conditions, which were more satisfactory for scientific observation than the medium usually allowed, the manifestations that took place were familiar, but could hardly be dismissed when so many were at a loss to explain them. The curtains of the spirit cabinet blew about, as if in a strong breeze, although the closed séance room was still and quiet. A zither that lay on the floor of the cabinet, well out of the medium's reach, began to play and at first repeated a single note over and over again, and then began to thump up and down on the floor. Finally, the instrument was seen leaving the cabinet and landing on the table in front of the sitters. During these and other happenings, the witnesses felt themselves pushed, pinched, patted, and even struck by what they described as a "large hand." Everyone agreed that Eusapia's hands were not only tightly held but were always clearly visible.

Word spread about this new round of séances and Eusapia's fame increased once again. Judging from the fact that she had allowed the test conditions in Paris to be much stricter than normal, she must have seen these sittings as a way to recover ground that she had lost when the SPR withdrew its support of her. If this was her plan, then she succeeded. Even in England, the Cambridge disaster was all but forgotten and it seemed that every scientist in Europe was anxious to have a séance with Eusapia Palladino.

Over the course of the next few years, Eusapia sat for one committee after another, but time was wearing on her and she was growing old. Sometimes, she was unable to perform and sometimes she found herself so exhausted after a séance that she was barely able to walk. The feeling of constantly being put to the test was starting to irritate her and it manifested itself as contempt for her sitters. She was tired, but she could not stop. The séance room was her workplace, and she had no other way to make a living.

In 1908, Eusapia performed in Naples for a three-man committee that was likely the most formidable that she had ever encountered. One of the men was Hereward Carrington, an American researcher who, though only 27 at the time, had been engaged in exposing fraudulent mediums for eight years and had written a book on their methods called *The Physical Phenomena of Spiritualism*. Carrington had persuaded the SPR -- despite their continued misgivings about Palladino - to allow the group's secretary, Everard Feilding, to accompany him to the séances. Feilding had little experience in the séance room, but he was skeptical of the paranormal. The third member of the committee was William Wortley Baggally, who had been investigating the paranormal for more than 30 years. He stated that he doubted that he had ever actually met a genuine medium and was an accomplished amateur magician who amused his

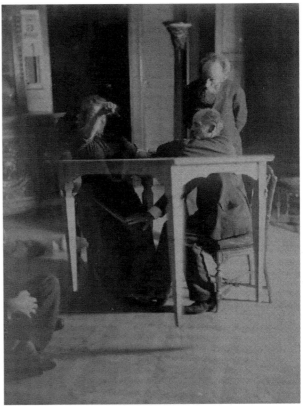

In 1908, Eusapia performed in Naples for one of the toughest committees she had ever faced, but they managed to find her abilities to be genuine.

friends and colleagues by duplicating the tricks of fraudulent Spiritualists.

The men were not presupposed to believe in spirit communication and Eusapia faced an uphill battle to convince them she was genuine. They planned to document everything to the letter. The séance records were taken by a shorthand stenographer and appeared in detail in Feilding's later book, *Sittings with Eusapia Palladino*

Hereward Carrington became one of Eusapia's biggest supporters but the tour he arranged for her in America ended with disaster.

& Other Studies. The records gave a minute-by-minute account of the researchers, extensive descriptions of the séance room and its furnishings, diagrams and measurements, and even careful notes on any changes in lighting. The phenomenon witnessed were not only noted but were classified and discussed in separate sections, but ample space was given for each investigator to note any disagreements that he might have and to state his own conclusions.

Throughout the sessions, the investigators reported movements and levitations of the séance table, movements of the cabinet curtains, bulging of the medium's dress, raps and bangs on the table, noises inside the cabinet, the plucking of a guitar, movements of a small table from the cabinet onto the séance table, movement and levitation of the small table outside the curtain, transportation of other objects from the cabinet, touches by unseen fingers and hands, appearances of hands from behind the curtain, appearances of heads and objects that looked like heads from the curtain, mysterious lights, sensation of a cold breeze issuing from a scar on the medium's brow, and the untying of knots. In short, it was an amazing night - which made the skeptical investigators more perplexed. They were baffled. They could find no easy explanation for what they had witnessed.

Their report of the strange events turned out to be a tremendous victory of Eusapia. Considering the newly gathered evidence, the SPR specifically withdrew its ban on Palladino and reasserted her place among mediums meriting serious investigation, in spite of her continued cheating. Most investigators, familiar with the medium and her trickery, felt that she was psychologically unable to discontinue it. Easily identified, they chose to ignore it because she also produced genuine phenomena at the same time.

One can hope that Eusapia enjoyed this small moment of glory, for it would be her last. By this time, her health was bad, and her séances were suffering because of it. Hereward Carrington was anxious to have her visit the United States so that his American colleagues might have the opportunity to witness her performances. Despite her failing health, she journeyed to America in 1909 and stayed for almost six months -- the most disastrous period of her career.

In her younger days, Eusapia would have loved the raw vibrancy and excitement of America. She would have seen it as a challenge, but by 1909, she was aging, tired, in poor health, and used to being taken seriously. However, the American press did not treat her as a visiting celebrity or even a scientific enigma. Instead, they saw her as a carnival sideshow and treated her more as an oddity than as a person who had stumped scientists in the major cities of Europe. She received many requests to perform but most of them came from music hall managers rather than from scientific committees. The prevailing attitude, from both the public and other mediums, seemed to be one of suspicion and hostility. Eusapia was very unhappy and soon became angry and difficult to work with. As proven at Cambridge, when Eusapia was unhappy, her séances suffered.

At first, she managed to get through them without much in the way of trickery. She performed 31 séances in America and Hereward Carrington oversaw 27 of them to prevent her from cheating. When she was under his controlled system, her physical mediumship continued to be impressive. But Carrington could not be present for her last four séances and that's when things went badly. Eusapia was sick, tired, and underestimated American audiences, who she felt were inexperienced. She did what she always did when phenomena was slow in developing - she cheated.

Unfortunately, two private detectives were in the audience one night and she was quickly exposed. Her acts of fraud received major press attention and irrevocably damaged her reputation in America. On May 10,

Was Eusapia Palladino the real thing - or a clever fraud?
We may never know the answer to that.

1910, a *New York Times* story appeared that stated, "In the séances held in this city recently, this greatest spiritualistic imposter in history was unmasked."

Her supporters rallied to her defense, but it did little good in America. In Europe, Eusapia continued to be regarded as a genuine wonder. As she had grown older, her powers had weakened, but it was generally regarded that she possessed genuine psychokinetic abilities. In time, the research into such abilities moved from the séance room to the laboratory. If she'd been tested properly, under strictly controlled conditions, in a laboratory setting, might scientists have gained more knowledge about psychokinesis and the paranormal?

But Eusapia Palladino didn't live to see those changes come about. When she left America, she went into retirement. There would be no further chances for science to explore the mysteries of this medium. She was an old, ailing woman now and she vanished into history. By the time she died on May 16, 1918, she was one of the most studied mediums in history, but she left an exasperating legacy behind. It's doubtful that the questions raised by her mediumship will ever really be answered.

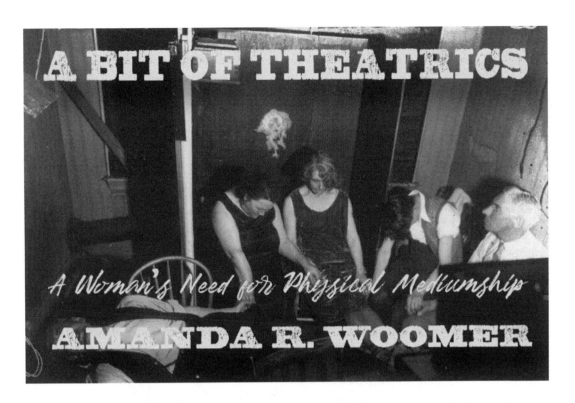

A BIT OF THEATRICS

A Woman's Need for Physical Mediumship

AMANDA R. WOOMER

"IT SEEMS ALL SPIRITS NEED THEATRICS, EH? EVEN CHRIST HIMSELF REQUIRES INCENSE AND HOLY WATER. WE'RE A SKEPTICAL PEOPLE. WE NEED CONVINCING."

—MEGAN CHANCE, *THE SPIRITUALIST*

Death. It is the looming inevitability that haunts all of us. And while many are blessed with blind faith that assures them that they know exactly what happens to themselves and their loved ones after they die, many more are not so lucky. For most people, doubt fills their thoughts on what waits for us on the other side of that last breath. Will we see the pearly gates? Will we be reborn as someone else? Will we linger near our loved ones, just out of reach? Or do we cease to exist?

Even in 2021–when people are filled with such certainty in their lives–they still question what happens after we die. No amount of technology or scientific breakthroughs over the centuries have come close to finding that answer for us. We don't know much more about the spirit world now

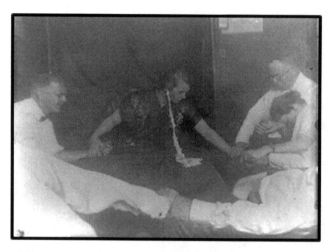

Mina Crandon (Margery) producing ectoplasm during a séance.

than we did in 1821... or 1921, for that matter.

Some find comfort in attending church in the hopes of saving their souls. Others collect as many gadgets as they can to hunt ghosts. And still, others pay to visit psychic mediums in the hope that they can peek behind the veil for a few minutes to see what they can expect when it's their turn to cross over.

Mediumship is a contested topic in today's day and age—not just in the paranormal world but in the mundane one as well. Charlatans hide among the genuinely gifted individuals, sometimes tainting the group as a whole. And yet, no matter how many frauds there may be, people have always flocked to psychics (and will probably always flock to them). As long as someone claims they can communicate with our dead loved ones, we'll be drawn to them... it seems to be part of our mortal nature.

Back when psychic mediums first appeared on the world's stage, they didn't just tell audience members that their loved ones were present—for who would pay to see a show like that? In the early days of mediumship, it was a performance for the masses, and these performers—whether truly gifted or not—knew that words were not enough to convince their audience that the spirit world was present all around them. They needed to show them in creative (and sometimes messy) ways.

When people think of the Victorian-Era Spiritualist Movement, they often imagine a group of finely dressed men and women surrounding a Ouija board with candles burning all around them. Throw in a few spirit trumpets, a flash of spirit photography, and you've got the perfect séance. Of course, it's a romanticized concept, and Ouija boards and Planchette writing was child's play when it came to physical mediumship in the Victorian and Edwardian-Eras.

In reality, objects were thrown through the air. Women were the ones in charge (many times performing in the nude). And above all else, the proof of a quality physical medium was the slimy presence of ectoplasm.

Ectoplasm is said to be a seemingly life-like substance that a medium will produce during a séance. It's been described by different individuals as "luminous spiderwebs" that solidify into various shapes (usually transforming into limbs ffipseudopodsffl, faces, or sometimes even entire bodies of a spirit). According to reports (of varying authenticity), the ectoplasm would extrude from the body, usually coming from one of the medium's orifices such as the mouth, ears, nose, and eyes. There are also many reports of ectoplasm seeping from the medium's navel, nipples, rectum, and vagina.

Not what you were expecting from the Victorian-Era? Well, Spiritualism shook the Victorians to their core, many times allowing women to become leaders, financially independent, and have a bit of autonomy. And in many women's

cases, ectoplasm was their ticket to notoriety in the world of mediumship.

While ectoplasm has made it into mainstream pop culture, there isn't any scientific evidence that it exists. Skeptics and scientists of the day declared that much of the ectoplasm photographed was fabricated from cheesecloth, gauze, and paper pulp. And yet, despite how fake many of the photos from séances appear (especially by today's standards), people clung to the idea that ectoplasm was an integral part of materialization during a séance. Even Sir Arthur Conan Doyle (author of Sherlock Holmes and Spiritualist advocate) wrote about this spooky substance, saying it was "a viscous, gelatinous substance which appeared to differ from every known form of matter in that it could solidify and be used for material purposes." Psychical researcher William J. Crawford, who studied physical mediumship, claimed

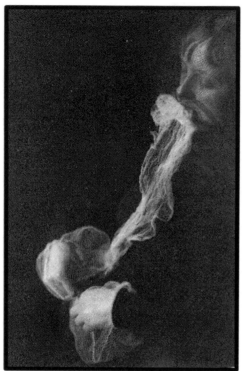

that "ectoplasm was the basis of all psychic phenomena."

In theory, spirits would take the ectoplasm created by their medium and drape it over their nonphysical body to be seen by those at the séance and move objects such as tables. Materialization was seen as the pinnacle of psychic ability in physical mediumship – it took a tremendous amount of concentration and even put the medium in harm's way. Producing ectoplasm was painful, and while the spirit materialized, it harnessed enormous amounts of energy, leaving the medium extremely vulnerable.

Despite this danger, the medium would willingly enter their cabinet in the séance room time and time again to make contact with the other side for those desperate to see a glimpse of the spirit world.

But... were these physical mediums truly in danger? Many psychical researchers (and even the staunch anti-Spiritualist, Harry Houdini) believed that the séance – even the supposed ectoplasm and vulnerability – was an elaborate performance.

Although some of the brightest minds of the day, including Nobel prize laureates, scientists, and physicians, did everything in their power to expose physical mediums as frauds, several theories were drafted by psychical researchers of the day to try to find a way to prove the existence of ectoplasm.

Some researchers believed that the human body contained an unidentified fluid called "psychode," which could be released from the body. This would explain levitating objects such as tables, chairs, and even people. According to the theory, this substance was invisible to the naked eye but could be touched and photographed.

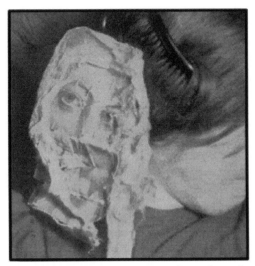

Eva C. with magazine cutout "ectoplasm."

Another theory to explain a medium's ability to conjure visages in their ectoplasm was "ideoplasty." This suggested that the faces produced were not the faces of a spirit present, but images from the medium's mind that would form in the ectoplasm. This idea still claimed that a medium could produce the supernatural substance and also helped defend some of the most prolific physical mediums of the day like Eva C., who supposedly conjured faces... also found in various magazines. Of course, Eva didn't actually cut those faces out and drape cheesecloth over them... she had read the magazine, and now her mind was conjuring the women's faces as a projected memory.

A censored photo of Eva C., naked during a séance.

Despite endless evidence against materialization and ectoplasm, physical mediums continued to shock audiences with their performances, constantly pushing the boundary of what women could do in the Spiritualist world.

Eva C. was known for performing séances only after being strip-searched and sewn into a skin-tight costume. Ectoplasm would ooze from her mouth, ears, nipples, and vagina. One séance produced a humanoid pseudopod from her vagina, spectators

Mina Crandon's (Margery) hand, most likely made of animal liver.

dubbing it the first (and most likely only) "pseudobirth."

Another famous physical medium from the 1920s was Mina Stinson Crandon, also known as Margery. She was a highly controversial medium of the 20th Century—her fans believed she was the greatest medium of all time while others saw her as a fraud and blamed her for nearly destroying psychical research in the United States. Ectoplasm would spill from her mouth, ears, and nose, though she also (supposedly) created a grotesquely formed hand that grew from her navel. Like Eva C., Margery produced pseudopods from between her legs that would ring bells, throw megaphones, and move tables. One

researcher believed she hid the fabricated ectoplasm in her vagina and pushed it out with muscle contractions (did we mention Margery liked to perform her séances in the nude?).

A young Irish Spiritualist, Kathleen Goligher, was another female physical medium known for her abilities in mediumship at a very young age. William J. Crawford began studying her in 1914 when she was only 16 years old. Kathleen was yet another medium that would produce "psychic rods" from her vagina, but unlike the psychode theory, Kathleen's rods could be seen, touched, and photographed. Other investigators visited Kathleen through the years to see her psychic rods for themselves, and by 1922, Kathleen was exposed as a fraud and retired from mediumship. Despite the allegations of fraud, early infrared photos were supposedly taken of her ectoplasm and psychic rods, but they were destroyed during World War II.

Spiritualism was a movement driven by women. High death rates from tragedies such as the Civil War and the Spanish Flu left wives and mothers grieving. Women in power such as Queen Victoria and Mary Todd

Lincoln are remembered for their public displays of grief, and their openness with their heartache allowed others to focus on grief, death, and what lay beyond. Women weren't just followers of Spiritualism, they were leaders, and mediumship was one of the few professions available to women at the time. These women were able to earn money, have influence (even over men), and find autonomy over their lives and bodies... and in the process, allowed others to connect with their dead loved ones on the other side.

Perhaps these physical mediums truly were gifted. After all, one researcher who studied Kathleen Goligher believed her early séances were genuine while the later ones were faked. This idea supports the theory that physical mediumship wanes as the individual gets older.

Or perhaps physical mediumship is all an elaborate hoax – simply a creative way to convince people that a spirit world does, in fact, exist and that world can manifest in our own. After all, humans are fickle creatures, and many times, we must see things to believe in them.

Is it possible that ectoplasm was a way to show those grieving that their loved ones aren't gone but simply

Kathleen Goligher, 1921

unseen? Can we judge those who were swept away by these women in the Spiritualist Movement – people who were simply trying to navigate their heartache? People desperate to connect with the other side? People searching for the spirit world?

After all, grief transcends time and space – it is the same in 2021 as it was in 1921. Who wouldn't want to find a way to reconnect with our loved ones who have gone one before us? Perhaps with a little help from a physical medium, a bit of theatrics, a darkened room, and a dash of ectoplasm, we might be able to see them again.

OUIJA, PEARL & PATIENCE

The Psychic Mystery of the Twentieth Century

APRIL SLAUGHTER

Ouija boards have long been the subject of intense spiritual fervor as well as scientific scrutiny. The subject of the 'game' often inspires a reaction of fear, as personal accounts and media portrayal have demonized the board, its use, and called into question the motivations of any sitter willing to place their hands on the planchette. But, it wasn't always so.

Spiritualism first took root on American soil with the revelations made by two sisters from upstate New York in 1848. Maggie and Kate Fox claimed they could communicate with the souls of the departed through a series of questions that were answered by raps on the walls and furniture. The intelligence of the responses led many to believe that the communications were genuine, and the Fox sisters were soon demonstrating these events for family, friends, and strangers alike. By the second half of the nineteenth century, word had spread of the success the sisters had with channeling, and a widespread fascination with spirit communication quickly blanketed much of the country.

Smithsonian magazine's article on the subject states, "Spiritualism worked for Americans: it was compatible with Christian dogma, meaning one could hold a séance on a Saturday night and have no qualms about going to church the next day. It was an acceptable, even wholesome activity to contact spirits at seances, through automatic writing, or table turning parties, in which participants would place their hands on a small table and watch it begin to shake and rattle, while they all declared that they weren't moving it."

Spiritualism also provided a link to the other side, a bit of solace to those who had lost loved ones to childbirth, disease, or death at war. Talking boards existed at the time, but businessmen looking to capitalize on the growing trend found a way to make it profitable as well. In 1890, Charles Kennard of Baltimore, Maryland pulled together a small group of investors to form the Kennard Novelty Company, which would manufacture and sell their talking boards exclusively to the eager public. The Ouija has been a part of American culture ever since.

Many people found their attempts at communicating with the dead entertaining, with little to no harm at all in using the Ouija board to facilitate them. Such was the case for two ordinary women in the infancy of the twentieth century.

In his book entitled *Patience Worth: A Psychic Mystery*, author Casper S. Yost wrote, "Upon a July evening in 1913 two women of St. Louis sat with a Ouija board upon their knees. Sometime before this a friend had aroused their interest in this unfathomable toy, and they had since whiled away many an hour with the inscrutable meanderings of the heart-shaped pointer; but, like thousands of others who had played with the instrument, they had found it, up to this date, but little more than a source of amused wonder... But upon this night they received a visitor. The pointer suddenly became endowed with an unusual agility, and with great rapidity presented this introduction: 'Many moons ago I lived. Again I come. Patience Worth is my name.'"

The women were baffled, and instantly obsessed with learning more from this seemingly intelligent entity that had suddenly begun to command their attention through the board. Immediately, they put pen to paper to make record of every communication they exchanged. Page after page of information was recorded in great detail.

Yost remarked, "Thus began an intimate association with 'Patience Worth' and a series of communications that in intellectual vigor and literary quality are virtually without precedent in the scant imaginative literature quoted in the chronicles of psychic phenomena... They include conversations, maxims, epigrams, allegories, tales, dramas, poems, all the way from sportive to religious, and even prayers, most of them of no little beauty and of a character that may reasonably be considered unique in literature."

The women who had been visited by Patience were Mrs. Pearl Curran and Mrs. Emily Grant Hutchings. Pearl was a housewife to the former Immigration Commissioner of Missouri, and Emily the wife of the Secretary of the Tower Grove Park Board in St. Louis. They were both bright, intelligent women. Mrs. Curran had never authored any sort of literature, but Mrs. Hutchings was a talented professional writer. In the beginning, it was suspected that perhaps Hutchings was somehow manifesting the communications, as they were so eloquently stated. It soon became apparent, however, that Mrs. Curran was the only individual required to be at the board when

Patience had something to say. It mattered not who the other individuals were that sat with her, and many had the opportunity to do so. Sittings would often include multiple people. The communications continued, and the messages continually involved.

Skeptics of the Ouija were (and remain) critical of the board, but several key factors had many of those witnessing the writing of Patience Worth believing the visitations were genuine. A typical sitting with the Ouija can be laborious, with the seemingly present entity intent on proving who they are, one letter at a time. More often than not, the messages have no real intellect behind them and often end as quickly as they began. Patience Worth never made any attempt to prove who she - or it- was. In fact, when pressed for details about her former life, she simply replied with cryptic messages like, "About me thou wouldst know much. Yesterday is dead. Let thy mind rest as to the past."

While not inclined to speak of herself in the past tense, Patience most notably spoke in an archaic English tongue, and only mentioned

An illustration showing the arrival of Patience Worth through Pearl's Ouija board

objects or events that existed during the seventeenth century or earlier. There were also times she used words that never had been used in the English language at any time in history. This fact alone would make the argument that Mrs. Curran 'invented' the entity a difficult one to prove or sustain. She simply did not possess the education or experience required to speak in such a manner.

Patience's knowledge of distinctly English things both fascinated and confused those attending the sittings. She often spoke of flowers and birds native to England, as well as the inner workings of the average English household generations beforehand, whether it be one of higher class and refinement, or one of the servants that worked for them. Even with this knowledge, however, Patience never made a reference or claim to having lived an English life.

One evening, a skeptical young doctor asked to converse with Patience. She did not hesitate to engage.

Doctor: I hope Patience Worth will come. I'd like to find out what her game is.

Patience: Dost then desire the plucking of another goose?

Doctor: By George, she is right there with the grease isn't she?

Patience: Enough to baste the last upon the spit.

Doctor: Well, that's quick wit for you. Pretty hard to catch her.

Patience: The salt of today will not serve to catch the bird of tomorrow.

It is also interesting to note that when these visitations occurred, they were done with all the gas lanterns lit, in full light, with none of the usual ceremony many associate with seances and other Spiritualist demonstrations. Patience was more than happy to engage, even while being challenged. No added effect was necessary.

During the initial months, Patience seemed more interested in holding conversations with her sitters. As time wore on, there would seldom be an evening where at least one poem had not been transcribed from the board, some rather lengthy and full of spiritual and mystical messages.

Ah, wake me not!
For should my dreaming work a spell to soothe
My troubled soul, wouldst thou deny me dreams?
Ah, wake me not!
If 'mong the leaves wherein the shadows lurk
I fancy conjured faces of my loved, long lost;
And if the clouds to me are sorrow's shroud;
And if I trick my sorrow, then, to hide
Beneath a smile; or build of wasted words
A key to wisdom's door—wouldst thou deny me?
Ah, let me dream!
The day may bring fresh sorrows,
But the night will bring new dreams.

Once this poem had been fully spelled out on the board, Mrs. Curran found herself in tears. Patience was quick to add another, as if to soothe her with a bit of added humor.

> *Patter, patter, briney drops,*
> *On my kerchief drying:*
> *Spatter, spatter, salty stream*
> *Down my poor cheeks flying.*
> *Brine enough to 'merse a ham,*
> *Salt enough to build a dam!*
> *Trickle, trickle, all ye can*
> *And wet my dry heart's aching.*
> *Sop, and sop, 'tis better so,*
> *For in dry soil flowers ne'er grow.*

In his book, Yost makes a point to show that any deception on the part of Pearl Curran is highly unlikely. He writes, "What evidence is there of their genuineness? Does Mrs. Curran, consciously or subconsciously, produce the matter? It is hardly credible that anyone able to write such poems would bother with a Ouija board to do it."

Indeed, it would have seemed quite a feat as Patience was able to author full-length novels with Pearl's assistance. *The Sorry Tale* was published in 1917 with stellar reviews. Her second novel *Hope Trueblood* did not quite see the success as the first when it was published the following year.

The words used, the references to distinctly English objects, along with an intellect no one could attribute to Pearl were all evidence of a kind that it would be nearly impossible for her to create such conversations and literature either with or without being conscious of it. She did not go into a trance state, nor did she have to exclusive attention to the board when the planchette was moving beneath her fingers. She often held conversations with others in the room while messages were being feverishly spelled out at the same moment.

She did what she could to press Patience for more personal information, but she was met with a stern resistance. She said, "I be like to the wind, and yea, like to it to blow me ever, yea, since time. Do ye to tether me unto today I blow me then tomorrow, and do ye to tether me unto tomorrow I blow me then today."

Pearl did not initially have the mind to monetize her unique situation. She didn't travel or set up any sort of public exhibition; it was all done within her circle of friends and other close associations within the Curran home. Over time, this changed. The sales from the novels had brought the Curran's a small amount of financial cushion, but by the 1920s, the interest

'OUIJA BOARD' AGAIN BRINGS MARVELOUS MYSTERIOUS MESSAGES

MRS. JOHN H. CURRAN

"Patience Worth," Mythical Character, Startles Literary World With Her Quaint English In Essays, Plays and Novels---Noted Writers Are Puzzled Over the Output of This Woman Supposed to Have Lived 300 Years Ago

in Spiritualism and in Patience herself had waned. John Curran had invested a hefty $4,000 on a Patience Worth-themed magazine that he was unable to sell or produce, thus leaving he and his wife with very little to live on.

John died in 1922, leaving Pearl alone to raise a child they had both adopted, along with a second that she would give birth to just six months following his death. Having little to no choice, Pearl decided to take her demonstrations to the public to earn enough to care for herself and her children. The widow married twice more, with her dedication and connection to Patience holding fast until a week before her death in 1937.

Mrs. Pearl Curran was buried, her headstone also bearing the name of Patience Worth.

This enduring mystery is one not easily proved or disproved, though many skeptics over time have attributed Pearl's conjurings as the product of a mentally ill mind. Some have argued that Mrs. Curran may have suffered from Dissociative Identity Disorder (more commonly known as Multiple Personality Disorder), but even with such a diagnosis, it is not common for more than one personality to be active at any given moment. Pearl was always able to carry on conversations independent of whatever the board, or Patience, was communicating.

The novel *To Have and Have Not* featured a character by the name of Patience Worth, and it had been published before Mrs. Curran had ever claimed to contact an entity of the same name. While this fact may have shed a shadow of doubt on the authenticity of the communications, it is hardly enough to vehemently dismiss them as fabrications.

Why Patience chose to channel her wisdom through Mrs. Pearl Curran, there is no explanation. Nor is there any evidence that she ever made herself known again using the board or anyone else at the helm. What is truly remarkable about Patience Worth and her ability and willingness to communicate through the Ouija is that her interactions were never of a distinctly negative or demonized nature, despite what many critics of talking boards would want the public to believe. The boards are a tool of intent... and any tool can be misused in the hands of someone intent on abusing the privilege. Mrs. Pearl Curran had no such intent. Rest well, Pearl. Let us hope we have not heard the last from Patience Worth.

"EVERYONE IS A MOON..."

Mark Twain's Vision of Death

SYLVIA SHULTS

"EVERYONE IS A MOON AND HAS A DARK SIDE WHICH HE NEVER SHOWS TO ANYBODY."

For Samuel Clemens, the writer better known as Mark Twain, part of that dark side was the loss of his brother, Henry.

Henry Clemens, the baby of the family, was a quiet, studious boy. In fact, Twain modeled Sid, Tom Sawyer's annoyingly well-behaved brother, on Henry. But Henry was no sanctimonious Sid Sawyer. He was handsome and generous, an all-around great guy, and everyone genuinely loved him. Henry worked at the same newspaper Twain did, and the brothers were close.

Twain even got Henry a job. Twain was a cub pilot on the steamboat *Pennsylvania*, which ran on the Mississippi River, on the popular route between St. Louis and New Orleans. Twain arranged a job for Henry as a "mud clerk". Mud clerks did anything that needed doing aboard the steamboat. They ran errands for the crew, carried messages, and did any job they were assigned. This was an unpaid position, but one from which Henry could work his way upward.

Around that time, in May or early June 1858, Twain had a deeply disturbing dream about his brother. It was the night before the *Pennsylvania* was scheduled to leave St. Louis on her run down to the Big Easy. He was spending the night at his older sister Pamela's house, and he dreamed that he was in the sitting-room of the house. A metallic coffin was supported on two chairs. Twain went closer, and was horrified to see Henry in the coffin, wearing one of Twain's suits. On his chest was a bouquet of white roses, with one red rose in the center.

Twain gasped himself awake, his heart pounding with adrenaline. The dream had seemed *so real.* Twain couldn't wrap his head around the fact that his unconscious mind could come up with something so horrifying, and so deeply personal. He clambered out of bed, still running on emotion. He couldn't go downstairs to the sitting-room to see Henry's dead body, he just couldn't face that yet, so he walked outside to clear his head. He walked an entire city block, he later wrote, "before it suddenly flashed on me that there was nothing real about this - it was only a dream." He came back to the house and shared the dream with Pamela, who reassured him that yes, it was only a dream.

Thankfully, Henry was alive and well. But there was trouble in the air. There was a pilot on board the *Pennsylvania* named William Brown, a bossy bully with a violent temper who had little use for the lowly mud clerks. He went out of his way to make Henry's life miserable. Finally, he accused Henry of not delivering a message, and hit him. Twain leapt to Henry's defense and beat the paste out of Brown. The captain broke up the fight, and offered to fire Brown. Twain arranged to return upriver on another steamboat, the *A.T. Lacey*. He told the captain he'd rejoin the *Pennsylvania* as soon as Brown was replaced. Twain left the *Pennsylvania* on June 5, and boarded the *A.T. Lacey*, which sailed two days after the *Pennsylvania*.

It was a fateful decision, and one that may very well have saved Twain's life. At 4 am on Sunday, June 13, the *Pennsylvania* was passing Ship Island, headed upriver, six miles below Memphis. She was pulling a flatboat loaded with wood. Many of the crew and most of the passengers were asleep when the boilers exploded, demolishing the front third of the boat.

Around half of the 500 people on board were killed instantly. Henry was blown off the ship, and suffered burns and internal injuries. Some stories say that the good-hearted Henry swam back to the ship and helped some victims escape the burning wreck. They were loaded onto the flatboat, which was then cut loose to escape the flames.

The *Imperial* was the first boat to arrive on the scene, and she took some victims to New Orleans. Others, including Henry, were rescued by the *Diana*, which took them to Memphis. People continued to die from the terrible injuries they'd suffered. Henry had inhaled superheated air, and his lungs were scorched.

Twain rushed to his brother's bedside. Henry fought his injuries for six days, aided by the attentive care of Memphis doctors. The nurses, too, doted on the good-looking kid, and did everything they could to make him comfortable. Henry responded well to the healing attention, and in just a few days, he seemed to be out of danger. But at 11 o'clock on the sixth night, a doctor told Twain that if Henry woke and couldn't get back to sleep, to ask the attending physician to administer 1/8 grain of morphine.

Henry did wake that night. The other victims moaned aloud in their pain, and Henry couldn't sleep. Twain told the medical student who had the overnight shift what the doctor had said. The student measured out the dose, but he may have gotten it wrong. Drugged by the accidental overdose of narcotics, Henry sank into a deep sleep. He died before dawn.

Word of Henry's heroics in the disaster had spread. Most of the wreck victims were being buried in plain wooden caskets, but the distraught ladies of Memphis took up a collection to buy Henry a fancy $100 metal coffin to honor his youth and his heroism. When Twain walked into the room in the Memphis Exchange building where Henry was laid out, he swayed on his feet, stunned with a chilling sense of familiarity. Henry was in his metal coffin, which was laid across two chairs. He was dressed in Twain's clothes - Twain hadn't realized that Henry had borrowed one of his suits, and the undertaker simply used the best clothes Henry had. On Henry's chest lay a bouquet of white roses. That was the only detail the dream had gotten wrong - there was no red rose among the white blooms.

But as Twain stood there, lost in his grief, an old woman came into the parlor and tucked a single red rose into the middle of the bouquet. The dream was complete.

The experience made a lasting impression on the young writer. Twain told and retold the story of Henry's death for the rest of his life. From being a skeptic, he made an about-face and embraced parapsychology with open arms. He was one of the first Americans to join the Society for Psychical Research when it was founded in London in 1882. He reached out to the group in the hope that the investigators could help him understand what had happened to him. He'd had a dream of the death of a loved one, which had then come true. He reeled from that experience for years. He could never quite escape the thought that if he'd known at the time how to interpret the awful dream, he could somehow have prevented Henry's death.

Even with his interest in psychical research, though, Twain was not about to fall prey to the nineteenth century craze for contacting the dead via mediumship. After watching a séance in San Francisco, he wrote a short story, "Among The Spiritualists", in which he unpacked his famously biting wit.

"There was an audience of about 400 ladies and gentlemen present, and plenty of newspaper people - neuters. I saw a good-looking, earnest-faced, pale-red-haired, neatly dressed, young woman standing on a little stage behind a small deal table with slender legs and no drawers - the table, understand me; I am writing in a hurry, but I do not desire to confound my description of the table with my description of the lady." In the story, Twain asked the medium, Ada Foye, to contact a friend of his with the utterly common last name of "Smith". And since this is Twain, he gave the séance a down-to-earth twist worthy of his plain-talking genius.

"I got hold of the right Smith at last - the particular Smith I was after - my dear, lost, lamented friend - and learned that he died a violent death. I feared as much. He said his wife talked him to death. Poor wretch!"

All kidding aside, though, Twain's life was forever changed by the loss of his favorite brother at such a young age. Twain's lifelong ruminating on the experience, though, formed his perspective on what happens after death. One of his sayings pokes gentle fun at the universal apprehension: "I do not fear death. I had been dead for billions and billions of years before I was born, and had not suffered the slightest inconvenience from it," he said.

SPIRITS *In the* MATERIAL WORLD

Within the walls of weathered but unwavering foundations, buildings grip their stories and secrets like the individuals who once inhabited them. Inanimate objects? Hardly. Buildings don't want their stories buried and forgotten under continuously mounting layers of time. As paranormal investigators and historians it's up to us to ensure that we breathe new life into the old, the weathered, the restless.

Public buildings become the cornerstones in the lives of many souls who were once associated with them, worked inside, lived in them or, in some cases arrived there after an untimely and sometimes gruesome end. The Vancouver Police Museum in Vancouver, British Columbia, is one such place. Built in 1932 and designed by Arthur J. Bird, the museum building once served as the city's Coroner's Court. It is the largest police museum in North America. Within its austere, authoritative walls, the three floors of the building witnessed many natural deaths, accidental deaths, murders, suicides and unsolved crimes.

BY GINA ARMSTRONG

The lab once housed several workers, lab technicians, analysts, and administrative staff. It's not a surprise that this is one of Vancouver's most haunted sites. The intriguing structure boasts a rich history and harbours several spirits who occasionally bob to the surface from beyond the realms of the otherworldly.

Museums are no exception when it comes to hauntings, paranormal energy or reminders that the past can choose to resurface at any given moment. In fact, the sheer nature of a museum is such that they, in fact, seem to promote hauntings. Displays of artefacts, collections of objects that people used daily, and the re-creation of authentic historic displays open the doors to a bygone era and can be a welcome mat encouraging ghostly activity.

The Police Museum's very foundation became cemented together over the years by the countless variety of energies of the individuals who passed through the building whether dead or alive. The dead and the living intermingled here. There was a constant ebb and flow of past and present intersecting with dark and light. This sifting of polar energy continuously occurred within the walls on a daily basis. It only makes sense that over decades, some of the more piercing fragments undoubtedly became embedded in the foundation.

Many of the key characters, though they have come and gone, still push vigorously through the veil to make themselves known. It's not so much unrest as it is, perhaps, a desire

PAULS FAMILY

to be acknowledged or, in some cases, hoping to be discovered. Death was a prevalent part of the Vancouver Police Museum's history and in addition to the Coroner's Court, the building was home to an Autopsy Suite, Morgue and City Analyst's Lab. Literally thousands of bodies made stops here before going to their final resting places. Apparently, some do not wish to rest or perhaps, simply can't rest because the narratives of their lives remain in limbo.

The bodies of the Pauls family who were the victims of Vancouver's first triple homicide, made their way through this building. In 1958, David, Helen and their 11-year-old daughter, Dorothy were brutally murdered and more than half a century later, there are still more questions than there are answers. The husband and wife, Russian immigrants, previously lived in Aldergrove, BC before purchasing their home in Vancouver in September of 1956.

The Pauls were an ordinary family with David working at the warehouse of the downtown Woodward's store and Helen worked evenings in a small sausage shop.

On the night of June 10th, David Pauls left their home sometime after 11:00pm to pick Helen up from her shift. He never made it. He was surprised by an attacker just outside the rear basement door, who shot him in the head but didn't instantly kill him. The murderer then used David's keys to enter the home. Young Dorothy was asleep upstairs where the attacker bludgeoned her to death and then returned to drag David to the basement and proceeded to beat him to death.

Helen Pauls was later reported by neighbours to have been seen running home from the bus stop in pouring rain around 11:30 that night as her husband clearly never made it to pick her up.

Helen only made it to her front hallway before she was shot and beaten to death. The motive for the murders was never certain though many theories were discussed over the years. David's wallet and vehicle were stolen, and Helen's purse was open but no-one could say for sure that anything was missing. Burglary was cited as a possibility, but some believed the attacker was, perhaps, someone who knew the Pauls because of the timing of the attacks. Did someone know their schedule and that Dorothy would be upstairs? The murderer also seemingly waited at the house for Helen.

In 1958 autopsies on the Pauls' corpses were performed at the current museum building. Their case remains unsolved and any clues as to the killer's identity remain a mystery.

Another cold case which has haunted police for close to 70 years has lingered in the shadows only to re-emerge recently. Two young boys, brothers, estimated at the time to be between the ages of six and ten, were found bludgeoned to death and buried in Vancouver's Stanley Park in 1953.

A groundskeeper discovered the remains and a few artefacts buried along with the bodies. It became known as The Babes in the Woods case. A hatchet was discovered with the bodies and police concluded this was the object which was used to kill the boys sometime around 1947. Their remains were concealed with a woman's coat and the corpses where positioned lying down with each of their soles facing each other. Not only has their killer never been found but the two young souls have never been identified so the victims, sadly, remain nameless. Stranger still, at the time of the murders, no missing persons were ever reported. Who and where was the mother of these children? There is speculation she may have somehow been involved.

Originally it was believed the bodies were that of a boy and a girl. The medical examiner at the time erroneously concluded that one of the victims was female. It wasn't until 1998 that a DNA test revealed both victims to be male. And though their killer or killers have never been discovered, there was new evidence which came to light in early 2021. Further forensic tests revealed that the brothers were, in fact, only half brothers. Encouragingly, there is now more to their story. The evidence that there are two different fathers opens

Exhibit C. Hatchet, found at the scene, identified as the murder weapon.

Exhibit B. Casts of [skulls] of two young children found in Stanley Park.

up many new possibilities. Police do believe that with modern technology and DNA, eventually the mother, both fathers and the boys will be identified.

For years, some of the boys' actual remains, skulls, bones, along with accompanying items were housed at the museum. Today replicas are displayed in their place along with plaques highlighting their tragic and unfinished story.

In as much as there were cases involving those who were unknown, there were also those who were well-known. The Morgue and Autopsy Room once housed the body of Hollywood actor, Errol Flynn who passed away in Vancouver, BC on October 14, 1959. His death wasn't particularly grisly but, instead, tinged with sadness. On the downturn of his amazing career and in financial need, Flynn came to Vancouver to sell his yacht. He met his demise after taking Demerol for some nagging pain. He was found unresponsive in the apartment of Dr. Grant

Gould who was the uncle to musician Glenn Gould. Flynn's autopsy was performed on one of the two stainless autopsy tables that can now be seen in the museum.

Due to the function of both the Autopsy Room and the Morgue, one might expect these rooms to be, in some way, dark, chilling or eerie. In fact, they are quite the opposite. The rooms were built with high ceilings. Funnelling structures taper into elaborate skylights above the autopsy tables. Here the cadavers would have been bathed in natural light which allowed for illumination while the coroner did the postmortem examinations. Though the two rooms are visually graphic, the overall ambience is not at all depressing.

It was because of cases such as the Pauls or The Babes in the Woods that the late Chief Coroner, Glen McDonald, an icon and eccentric personality believed that work he did on the dead was to help protect the living. During the early days of the Coroner's Court, next to the morgue, many inquests took place where McDonald delved into the circumstances of the deaths of hundreds of individuals. In the basement of the facility there was The Blood Room, Overflow Morgue, and the Forensic Lab.

In addition to his work in the Morgue and Autopsy Room, McDonald believed that the general public, not just police or medical personnel, could learn from the dead. McDonald felt it was his duty to educate the living and, with the help of his colleague, George Shoebottom, McDonald and his travelling museum hit the road. With various specimens of hearts, lungs and tissue samples from autopsies preserved in formaldehyde, his Travelling Wax Museum was born and made its way to the public. It featured a brain with a gunshot wound, a stabbed heart, a smoker's lung and

much, much more. The visual nature of the exhibit captured audiences and taught them about the human body. The exhibit also sparked lively academic and casual conversations around the taboo topic of death.

Even as recently as the 1970's and into the 1980's the macabre specimen exhibit travelled across the province to luncheon meetings, high schools, BC's Pacific National Exhibition (PNE) and even made its way to the Chamber of Commerce. For 300 years, human dissection played an important part in the advancement of Western medicine and McDonald felt his travelling show could teach the living about diseases, accidents and even grisly murders. Though the travelling specimens are

The Travelling Wax Museum
Right -- **Chief** Coroner Glen McDonald

no longer in rotation, they can be viewed as part of a permanent true crime exhibit in the Vancouver Police Museum.

While scientific data is paramount in criminal investigations, the paranormal hovers on the fringes where data can't always be isolated to experiences involving your eyes, ears or brain. Ghosts, their presences and their manifestations defy scientific paradigms. Things ghosts can do are truly supernatural. They can appear as mists, shadows, orbs, or as material human beings. They can move things and make sounds without bodies. They can cause atmospheric changes in a room or elicit emotional responses from the living. Evidence shows that spirits often pull their energy from the

vitality around them. Living, breathing human beings can lend ethereal beings this energy as can electrical equipment or appliances. Similarly, a building or location which encompasses remnants of vigorous activity or harbours energy from the past can potentially help to fuel paranormal activity.

It's not a surprise, considering the building's history, ghostly incidents are reported by visitors and staff at the Vancouver Police Museum. Paranormal groups have explored the museum over the years to investigate hauntings. Several reports include the sounds of children. One individual heard a girl's voice during a recording session. Another person reported hearing wet feet running in the Autopsy Room and described it sounded like a young child running. On other occasions there have been reports of seemingly mischievous door slamming or sounds as if doors were being latched. Could these be ghosts of children whose bodies ended up here?

The Vancouver Police Museum's mystique in not only in the hauntings but also lies in the fact that the basement is not routinely open to the public. Suspended in the darkened rooms, several artefacts remain, and time stands still showcasing various stages of the museum's history. One area predominantly has antique glassware, bottles, test tubes and containers – some of which still have chemicals in them. There are shelves tucked into long corridors where old books, photos and ephemera are preserved in temperature-controlled rooms. In the heart of the lab, old microscopes sit stooped over the tables like small ancient dinosaurs, bodies covered in their own little plastic body bags.

The bottom floor of the building was in use until 1996. The staff of the Forensic Lab were the last of the daily human bustle to vacate the building. Most of the items sit exactly where they were left and like a snapshot, the

Office of John Vance, "Canada's Sherlock Holmes"

final moments of the lab remain here like an eerie still life.

Back in its heyday, the forensic lab in the basement was the working home to Vancouver's Inspector John Vance, who became known as "Canada's Sherlock Holmes" during the 1920's-30's. Inspector Vance was an extraordinary pioneer. Independently he developed forensic science techniques and became well-known across all of North America. He was so proficient at his job that there were several attempts on his life during the 1930's as Vance delved into the waves of corruption and crime in Vancouver.

Vance was an expert in gathering trace evidence, reasoning, toxicology, firearms examination and serology. He originally started out as a city analyst for the city of Vancouver ensuring the safety of food, water, alcohol and various items for public consumption. He was believed to be one of the only people even doing forensic analysis in the 1920's in Canada, possibly North America.

The Vancouver Police Museum building's origin story is more fascinating because of the work done by John F.C.B. Vance. In 1914, Vance was contacted by the Vancouver Police to aid in the case of a missing woman, Clara Millard. Vance took various items and samples from the Millards' home and was able to confirm traces of blood at the scene. The Millards' houseboy was eventually arrested and convicted of manslaughter.

Once police recognized the value of science as a part of the analysis process, Inspector Vance was consistently called upon to help aid in crime investigations. From burglaries to murders, Vance helped to solve countless crimes in and around the Vancouver area using unprecedented forensic techniques. He even invented his own tool – a portable ultraviolet lamp which could detect traces of

bodily fluids! He soon outgrew the lab at Vancouver Police Headquarters and needed more space. Hence, his introduction to the museum building around 1934 when a new lab was built to his specifications. Vance spent many days juggling his job of food inspector along with forging a bond with the Vancouver Police as he worked tirelessly alongside the technicians and analysts at the Coroner's Court.

The professional climate in the Coroner's Court was highly irregular and extremely innovative. With all of the facets of crime solving under one roof, the level of communication and activity around investigations was charged with energy, excitement, teamwork and integration which took collaborative crime solving to new heights. With Vance's expertise and new state-of-the-art equipment, the City Analyst's Lab was one of the most, if not the most advanced not only in Canada but in all of North America. Here inclusiveness was also cutting edge. Minorities, diverse ethnic groups and women were hired into prominent positions during a time when predominately white men ruled the fields of science and policing.

Vance's contribution to forensic science was truly extraordinary and when he retired in 1949, his legacy continued with the hard work of his successors George Fennel and Inspector Percy Easler.

In the 1980's new forensics techniques including DNA profiling were introduced. And though a major breakthrough in criminal investigations, new DNA equipment was very expensive. This proved to be detrimental to the Analyst Lab's future as a dilemma arose of whether to update a space that previously had very little renovations during its course. For decades the lab stood pretty much in the original layout designed by Vance. By 1996 most DNA analysis was outsourced to private labs or to the RCMP. So the lab which once rivalled even the best FBI labs in the country slowly became out of date. Instead of costly upgrades the decision was made to shut it down.

The Vancouver Police Museum moved into the building shortly after. It proudly houses true crime exhibits, history on Vancouver's traffic laws, displays radio equipment, has a weapons room, tissue and organ samples and stores many archival documents. Truly engrossing but not for the faint of heart. Visitors get a comprehensive feel for what sort of work was being done and the significance the building played in the development of novel methods for solving some of the most notorious cases in BC history.

The rooms may not be packed with people as they once were, but the building does welcome many visitors throughout the year. The general public has the opportunity to step back in time and to be temporarily immersed in history brimming with colourful characters during Vancouver's coming of age. The Autopsy Room still showcases a bullet hole in one of the windows. The displays featuring some unsolved cases also leave a lasting impression. These are stories of people whose tragedies, like the ghosts, still haunt us.

Recently there we were three paranormal groups on site together. While conducting an experiment in an attempt to see if there were any spirits who wanted to communicate, a small device standing upright eased its way to a flat position on one of the autopsy tables. It didn't simply fall over but gradually and slowly slid downward. This happened not once, but three times. Each time while being prompted. The activity was caught on camera.

An individual from one group also captured a moaning sound and voices between the opening of the Morgue and Autopsy Room. This same area also recorded prominent electromagnetic spikes.

Finally, there is the dark and curious basement. Here there are unexplained sounds, dusty corners and a feeling of general unease but most of this is likely one's imagination sparked by being intimately surrounded by so many whispers of the past. A chalkboard which long ago served its purpose, still with names of employees, hangs on the wall. It is illuminated by a couple of dimly lit lights. But when it comes to paranormal activity the museum staff insist they prefer to be kept in the dark. The basement serves as the main exit workers and volunteers must take at the end of their shifts, sometimes very late at night.

For those of us who are mesmerized by the paranormal and enthralled by history, The Vancouver Police Museum has it all–riveting anecdotes, exhibits with a touch of gore, a sprinkle of Hollywood glitz, true crime, mysterious cold cases, engaging displays and a few persistent ghosts. After a visit it's a place you leave but that doesn't necessarily leave you.

Glen McDonald's goal was to educate the public and to help protect

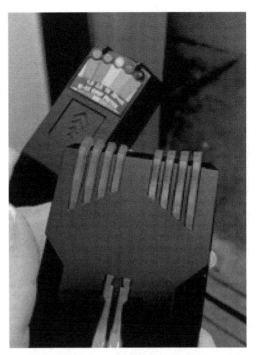

Electromagnetic Field Meters (EMF) used in paranormal investigations

the living. The stories of those who made incredible contributions to Vancouver's crime solving history like McDonald, Inspector Vance, and George Fennel, come to life at the Police Museum. Inside this building their work still continues. It is because of their passionate dedication and the meticulous preservation efforts of the museum we have hope that one day some of these cold cases will, indeed, be solved.

Though exact scientific methods are not part of the paranormal tool kit, as paranormal investigators and

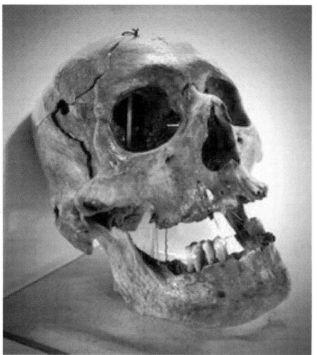

And similar to those in the field of science, paranormal investigators can continue to engage the public in conversations around death and the complex and compelling theories about what happens after we die. We know there is much more to unearth when it comes to understanding why some places are haunted and why some ghosts remain among the living. Through a combination of historic and paranormal research we can attempt to seek these types of answers. We can also honour the memories of those whose lives have not quite reached their conclusions. In the end, the goals of the paranormal investigator don't stray far from those who once used scientific innovation to solve crimes. We hope the voices of the dead can help educate the living. In due course, we also hope that by sharing the stories of those who aren't able to move on we can not only grant them peace, but in some cases, finally give them a name.

historians we continue our research of the spirit world using a vast array of methods to attempt to explain the unexplainable. Human beings seem to be fearful, uncomfortable but endlessly captivated with the subject of death and the afterlife.

Research methods of paranormal investigators are not quite mainstream but as we have seen, history is built on innovation. We can use paranormal investigation in an attempt to reach the spirit world in order to learn about those who passed. Maybe one day it will be another way to get answers to questions that are shrouded in mystery.

Photos by Victoria Vancek
Photo of Glen McDonald courtesy of Vancouver Archives

The Greatest Cave Explorer Ever Known

THE GHOST OF FLOYD COLLINS

KARI BERGEN

This story takes place twenty years ago in October of 2001. I was 16 years old, just months past my last chemotherapy treatment and traveling with my mom to Florida to visit my grandfather and attend my grandmother's memorial. My grandparent's house still looked much as it had the last time I had come to visit, Grandma's mix of southwest curios and beach vibes still on display. But it felt strange to me right away as Grandpa made it clear he wanted us to sleep in the master bedroom on what used to be his and Grandma's bed. He'd been sleeping out on a couch in the living room since Grandma passed. I was a little unnerved by the idea of sleeping there, so I tried to suggest that I would be most comfortable in the guest room. Still, he insisted that we take the room.

Grandpa has always been particular about what you do with your luggage when you come to stay. "Aren't you going to stay the night?", he would joke as he showed you which drawers to unpack your suitcase into. This time was no different and he had me unpack my clothes into Grandma's now nearly empty dresser drawers. I carried my shower bag into the bathroom which is attached to the bedroom by a short hallway with walk-in closets on either side. As I reentered the bedroom just moments later, I noticed one of Grandma's dresser drawers was open.

"Huh. That's weird," I thought. "I don't remember opening that drawer." The bottom two drawers were still filled with Grandma's things. But without giving it much more thought I shut the drawer and went out to join the family in the living room.

Later that evening, I went into the room to grab a sweater and that same drawer was open again. I still wasn't thinking too much about it, but I began paying attention to that drawer every time I came into the room. It happened several more times that night and I began to wonder who was coming in to open it -- and why?

That night I woke up from sleep to use the bathroom and although I had made quite certain that the drawer was closed when I had gone to bed, the drawer was now cracked open an inch or so. I got out of bed and went down the tiny hall to the bathroom. When I returned, to my dismay, the drawer was now wide open. "MOM! MOM! ARE YOU OPENING THIS DRAWER?!" I startled her awake with my accusations.

"What drawer?" she asked, half asleep.

"This one!" I pointed emphatically.

"No," she squinted at me. Of course, she hadn't been sneaking around opening that drawer every time I closed it.

The next morning, I was determined to try and prove to my Mom that I wasn't crazy -- the drawer was opening on its own. So, when we left the house for brunch, Mom and I both carefully made sure the drawer was closed and shut the bedroom door behind us as we left. We were gone for only a few hours and the first thing we did when we got back to the house was check on that drawer. I couldn't believe my eyes! The drawer had opened as wide as it would go! I began to think it must be my Grandma, trying to get my attention.

I was chatting about it on the porch with my Mom later that evening and Grandpa came out looking upset. "Who's going through Grandma's things?" he asked us. Mom and I looked at each other, "No one, what do you mean?" He proceeded to tell us that he kept finding her drawer open. It upset him that it was being left open and he asked us to let him know if we wanted to look through her things. We decided to look through the drawer right then. It was mostly full of costume jewelry and old handbags but at the bottom of the drawer was Grandma's wallet with all her personal documents and some items that Grandpa had been searching all over the house for. He was so relieved that we'd found them. I didn't tell him it was Grandma who showed us where it was.

Grandpa goes to bed early every night, and since he was sleeping on the living room couch this meant Mom and I would go read in bed every night around 9 pm. That night, we were reading side by side, when I happened to look up and see my Grandmother's portrait hanging on the wall. The shadows seemed to be shifting, making her eyes move. *You're imagining that* I thought and turned my gaze back to my book. But by the end of the next page, I couldn't help but glance back up. AHH! She was looking right at me, and her face was definitely moving!

"Mom, does that picture look like it's moving to you?!" I asked her. She looked up from her book and gasped as the face and eyes on the portrait turned to look back at her. "YES!" she exclaimed, "and her mouth is moving!"

It was then that I noticed that it looked like Grandma's portrait was speaking. We were both severely creeped out. But at the same time, it was Grandma, so we talked to her and told her we loved her, that we knew she was there, and we appreciated the visit. That night we both had visitation dreams in which we spent time with Grandma. I dreamed that I was walking around one of Grandma's favorite places, Silver Springs, with her by my side.

The following morning Grandpa again came to us looking upset. "Who's been going in Grandma's Office during the night?" he wanted to know.

Neither of us had been inside because he had asked us specifically not to go in there (where her ashes were) and to stay off Grandma's computer. "I know someone's been in there because the door was open, the lights and computer were on..." he said, looking hurt.

Mom and I looked at each other in surprise. "Grandpa, none of us have been in the office, I promise," I tried to assure him. It soon became clear that Grandma was the one going in and out of the office when Grandpa came to us a few days later with tears in his eyes and told us he'd found the computer turned on, logged onto the internet, (which took more than the simple click of a button in 2001), signed into Grandma's email, and opened to the last email Grandma had ever sent. It

was a message to her best friend saying she was going back into the hospital and didn't think she would make it. He didn't understand how it had happened because no one, not even Grandpa, knew the password to access her email.

So, it was after a week of undeniable contact with the spirit world that we began our two-day trip back to our home state of Illinois. Our plan was to take our time heading back, stopping for a tour at Mammoth Cave in Kentucky and doing some antiquing along the route home.

The door to the spirit world seemed to have been flung open by our shared experiences in Florida. We spent the entire first day of the drive talking about all things paranormal and stopping at just about every roadside antique store we could spot from the highway. We ended up stopping near Chattanooga for the night with only three and a half hours to drive the next day until we reached Mammoth Cave.

I've always been interested in caves. On one hand I find them deeply beautiful and fascinating, on the other, dangerous and absolutely terrifying. As with just about anything that fascinates and terrifies me, I always want to learn more about

THIS TIME I WANTED TO TAKE THE LANTERN TOUR SO I COULD ASK THE GUIDE FOR GHOST STORIES. IT WAS OCTOBER AFTER ALL.

them. I had been to Mammoth Cave for a regular tour earlier in the year, but this time I wanted to take the lantern tour so I could ask the guide for ghost stories. It was October after all.

We ended up getting a late start the next morning and didn't hit the road until after lunch. By the time we started seeing signs for Mammoth Cave it was already 3:30 pm. Following the road signs for Mammoth Cave, we got off Highway 65 at Cave City and continued following the signs to Mammoth Cave Road. Everything we passed looked old, and the creepy vibes were just getting me more excited. My excitement quickly faded as we approached the visitors center and I realized they were on an off-season schedule. We had arrived too late for the lantern tour. My disappointment lasted for only a few minutes, until I suddenly remembered the rock shop we had passed on the way in, and we decided to adventure there instead.

Big Mike's Rock Shop looked exactly like my kind of absurd roadside kitsch, with a giant Mosasaurus sculpture in the parking lot and signs advertising "Big Mike's

Mystery House... an oddity you won't want to miss." *This will be wonderfully ridiculous,* I thought.

We looked through the rocks in the parking lot then went inside. It turned out that Big Mike had passed away a few years prior so there was no one to give us a tour of the mystery house. The woman that was running the rock shop offered to let us wander the house ourselves, but it gave me the creeps, so I declined to go in by myself. We spent the next half an hour browsing the rocks and crystals and I bought a few after the woman convinced us that we needed some for spiritual protection. Now it was about 4:30 pm. What next? I had seen signs for antiques in Cave City, so I suggested we go check them out.

I don't know what Cave City is like during peak season, but on this late October evening it was like a ghost town. We were the only car on the streets, and we weren't seeing any people around town. Everything seemed to have closed at 4 and we felt eerily out of place. We were just about to give up when we found what seemed like the only open shop in Cave

City, an antique store on Broadway Street. The place was a bit creepy even for me. Since they were closing soon half the lights had been turned off. The dimly lit booths were housed in chain link cages, half of which were padlocked shut. and several of which contained tableaus of mannequins wearing vintage clothes. We got through there pretty fast.

By this time, it was already getting dark, and we decided to be done traveling for the day. We got some dinner at the only place that seemed open, which was a Cracker Barrel near the highway. Afterwards, we decided to check into the nearby Cave City Comfort Inn Hotel. Sure, the parking lot seemed a little empty, but it looked like a perfectly normal hotel from the outside. We walked into a darkened lobby, the only lights coming from the check in desk. All the furniture, entryways, everything except for the check-in desk and elevator were draped in plastic. "Is it even open?" I wondered.

We were just about to give up standing awkwardly in the dark and find a different hotel when the front desk girl shows up. She's very nice and in no time, we are up in our room relaxing. We spend a little time reading but we are very tired, and the lights are out by 9 pm.

The next thing I know I am startled awake by Mom as she turns on the light. "Wake up. We have to go, I can't sleep in this bed one more minute," she said, looking nearly zombie-like with exhaustion.

"What? It's 1 o'clock in the morning! You want to leave now?" I'm not thrilled with this idea but the look on her face has me already up and packing my bag. The beds were rock hard, and her back was bad. She couldn't take it anymore.

Moments later we were down in the dark lobby waiting for the front desk girl to check us out. She looked concerned, "You want to check out now? May I ask why?"

We explained the hard bed situation and she was very sympathetic. "Oh! Well... if you don't mind sharing a King bed, we do have one room upstairs that has a brand new mattress on it. It should be softer than the one you were on if you want to try it." We didn't really want to start driving in the middle of the night with no sleep, so we gratefully said yes to the room.

I've never had the hotel staff escort me to my room before, but that's exactly what she did. She disappeared for a moment and then came out from behind the desk with a room key. She began chatting to us in the elevator, only revealing once we stepped out onto the 3rd floor that the whole floor was under construction. All the rooms on this floor, except for ours, were gutted and awaiting renovation. She's chatting away as we follow down the hall behind her. As we approach a particular room I have an overwhelmingly intense feeling of unease, "I hope it isn't that one," I shudder. I am inexplicably relieved when we keep walking past it.

"Oh! I almost missed it!" she barely stops talking as she backs up to open the very door that I was afraid of.

Front desk girl is still chatting as she inserts the room key and opens the door. She only opened the door about 6 or 8 inches when she seemed to see something and gasped, "Oh, excuse me!" She quickly pulled the door shut. Her eyes darted to ours with a look of fear and confusion. After half a second, though, she shook it off. "That light shouldn't be on..." she said, sounding unsure, "but there can't be anybody in this room."

It sounded like she was trying hard to convince herself.

She unlocked and opened the door again but wouldn't enter. She stood in the doorway, her back pressed up against the door and pointed to the other side of the room. "There's a pull-out couch and some extra blankets in that chest if you need them," she told us.

My eyes followed her hand. I took one look at the furniture and for no outwardly discernible reason, it sent a shiver of horror down my spine. Our gracious front desk lady made a very speedy retreat and before I could even process what I was feeling she was gone.

This room had a presence that was giving me such a strange sense of foreboding that I didn't even change back into my pajamas before hopping into the bed and throwing the covers up over my head. If this was the only room in the hotel with a bed good enough for Mom's back, then I would just have to ignore it. It took a while for me to relax enough to fall asleep. I couldn't shake the feeling that if I were to take the blanket off my head and look, I would see someone there staring back at me.

Finally, I drifted off to sleep and immediately began dreaming. In my dream a frail-looking old man in worn clothes was standing at the foot of the bed staring at me. I couldn't see his eyes because they were so sunken.

They seemed to disappear into pools of darkness, but I was sure they were looking at me. I woke up with a start, still under the safety of my blanket. I was spooked but glad I had woken myself up from that awful dream.

I drifted back to sleep and was once again back inside the same dream, only this time he was closer, sitting on the end of the bed, still staring. I woke up again drenched in a cold sweat. This continued to happen all night long. Every time I would fall back asleep, I would find myself stuck in the same dream and every time he came closer and closer. Soon he was standing near the head of the bed, and I could hear him whispering loudly, "I'm under the rocks. I'm under the rocks."

I was feeling increasingly panicked each time I woke up. In the final dream he was bent down close to my face, just on the other side of my blanket shield, so close I could smell his putrid breath. Every time he whispered, "I'm under the rocks" it smelled of cloying, musty, wet stone and earth with a hint of old decay.

That was it! As I woke up from this final dream, I threw the blanket off and began to get out of bed. Apparently, Mom had the same thought because she woke up and threw off the covers at exactly the same time I did. Wordlessly we readied ourselves to leave and checked out of the hotel after getting less than 6 hours of "sleep." We left so fast we didn't even get our complementary morning coffee.

It wasn't until we were a few miles down the highway heading home that either of us finally spoke. "Was there something *weird* about that hotel room?" I finally asked Mom.

"YES!", she said immediately. "Did you see that stain on the wall?"

No, I hadn't, but to be honest I was so disturbed by the room that I intentionally hadn't looked around. I was afraid of what I would see. Mom proceeded to tell me that she saw a large "bloody" looking stain on the wall behind the pull-out couch. She didn't get any sleep all night because she kept being awakened by an old man who was sitting on the bed and whispering, "I'm under the rocks."

I wish I had a picture of the horrified look on my face. I was expecting her to say that she didn't notice anything unusual about the hotel room but instead she confirmed everything I'd experienced.

It was such a strange and memorable experience that 20 years later I still think about it. Who was he?

Why was he reaching out to us? Was he really "under the rocks" somewhere?

I had tried a few times over the years to see if I could find any information about the hotel that would help explain my experience, but I never found anything. Mom and I had always supposed that maybe someone had died in that room and that's why it was the only room in the whole hotel with a brand-new mattress. But if it was someone who died in the hotel room, why would they keep telling me they are "under the rocks"?

It wasn't until I started looking into the history of Cave City while writing this article that I realized my dream may have some very interesting connections to local history. I was unaware at the time, but it turns out there is a well-known local story of a man named Floyd Collins being trapped *under the rocks* in nearby Sand Cave.

What a coincidence!

I just had to look into this story and I promptly ordered and read a copy of a book called *Trapped!: The Story of Floyd Collins* by authors Robert K. Murray & Roger W. Brucker. Published in 1979, it still seemed like the best resource I could get my hands on to learn about Floyd

Floyd Collins was called the "Greatest Cave Explorer Ever Known" when he began developing caves in Kentucky in the early 1900s.

and his entrapment. Especially since the authors took the time to dispel the many myths and untruths surrounding Floyd's story and are some of the few people to ever have been allowed into Sand Cave after it was sealed. All the quotes and dialogue in my retelling of Floyd's story are taken from the book *Trapped!* and the sources they quote.

William Floyd Collins, "Greatest Cave Explorer Ever Known", was born June 20th, 1887, and spent nearly his whole life exploring the vast interconnected cave systems in and around the Mammoth Cave area. The

Collins were a farming family that worked together to grow grains, fruits and vegetables on their 200-acre farm located on Flint Ridge, just a few miles from the entrance to Mammoth Cave. It was there that little Floyd developed his early fondness for caves, exploring nearby Buzzard Cave with his siblings just 1,000 feet from the Collins family home.

By the age of six, Floyd was already wandering into Salt Cave all alone and wriggling himself into every crack and crevice he could find. As Floyd got older, he became so engrossed with his caving activities that he would often arrive late or skip class at the local one-room schoolhouse. His classmates remembered him as a daredevil who wasn't afraid of taking big risks. If someone suggested that something he was doing was dangerous, he would just laugh in their face. His love for caves bordered on obsession.

Floyd continued to avidly explore the area's caves throughout his teenage years and into young adulthood, but for the most part caving was his beloved pastime. He still earned most of his income working hard on the family farm, and by the age of 23, had saved enough money to buy 30 acres of his own land

which adjoined his father's. Floyd was thrilled to discover a small cave on his land which he named, "Floyd's Cave". It wasn't a very beautiful cave, but it did contain some rock formations which Floyd sold to tourists, whetting his appetite for hunting down his own commercial sized cavern.

Although the Collins' farm fared better than some of the others in the area, it was tough going scratching out a living. The limestone filled karst landscape of the region provided a poor quality of rocky soil and less than ideal conditions for farming. Taking advantage of Mammoth Cave's tourism and operating a commercial cave business remained the most lucrative option for many of the area's landowners.

Floyd got his first taste of "professional" caving in 1912, when he was hired by Edmund Turner to guide him through Salts Cave, earning himself one dollar a day. Up until this point Floyd's caving knowledge was based purely on a mixture of his firsthand experience and superstitions. With Turner, he began to understand some of the Geology and scientific information about the caves he so loved. His time with Turner, and Turner's discovery of Great Onyx cave, greatly inspired

Floyd and further stoked his ambitions for discovering his own profitable cave. By the outbreak of World War I, Floyd was spending most of his time either mining Great Onyx for tourist souvenirs or exploring caves for new passageways.

Great Onyx Cave, where Floyd worked as a guide before discovering his own commercial cave.

While out trapping on the family property during the bitter winter of 1916-17, Floyd found that one of his traps had been dragged into a crevice by a trapped animal. He examined the crack and because of the way it "breathed," felt confident that there must be a big cave on the other side. Before he explored anything, Floyd went to his father, and nonchalantly asked him if he would be willing to split the profits if he could find a commercial-sized cave on the property. Although Floyd's Father, Leonidas or "Lee," would later claim that caving was "in the blood," he himself never really put much stock in it as a profession. But Lee didn't mind the extra money, so he agreed to it in a written contract that Floyd insisted upon. Floyd had seen what feuds in the "Cave Wars" had done to other families in the area and he wanted to

have everything in writing from the start.

The "Cave Wars" flared up after Mammoth Cave became part of the National Park Service and locals who lived nearby began to desperately want to get into cave promotion. Soon, they began advertising and conducting tours of their own caves, located on their own property - even though most of them were simply parts of the much larger Mammoth Cave. At that time however, people either didn't suspect this, or just didn't care. If a person had an entrance to a cave on his property, then he had his own cave. The caves were advertised and marketed wildly, and each owner would extol the virtues of his cave above all the others in the area. Each

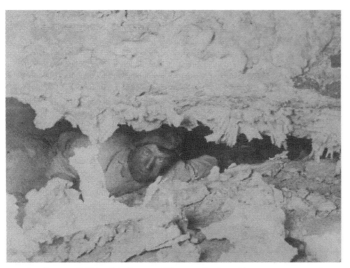
A photo of Floyd taken while exploring the passages of Crystal Cave. It was used for publicity purposes at the time.

cave to a tourist being killed there in an accident.

On a few occasions, the visitors themselves even got into the act. One incident involved rival caves that were located right next to one another. A fence separated the two entrances and as visitors filed into each cave for a tour, the owners encouraged them to throw rocks at the opposite tour group.

The "Wars" had been tough on friends and neighbors and Floyd didn't want that to affect his family, so a contract, even with his own father, was crucial to success.

Floyd resumed his explorations and after several weeks of hard labor clearing passages, he came upon a 65-foot room with white and cream-colored gypsum "flowers" encrusting the walls. Floyd named it "Wonder Cave," but its official name became Crystal Cave after the gypsum formations, a name suggested by Floyd's neighbor, William Travis Blair.

Soon, the whole Collins family became involved in developing the cave for commercial use. They spent a back-breaking twelve months enlarging the entrance, smoothing the

would post as many signs as possible between major roads and the entrance to Mammoth Cave, hoping to lure travelers away from the most popular attraction.

Sometimes the competition between the operating caves became more than just who did the most advertising. On many occasions, violence and vandalism marred the countryside. Signs were torn down and destroyed, fires were set, and even shots were occasionally fired. Word of mouth was sometimes just as destructive. The owners of caves often told visitors who came to see them that they shouldn't visit another nearby attraction for a variety of reasons, ranging from poison gases in the rival floors into trails, filling holes, building stairways, and of course, putting signs out on the road to Mammoth advertising the opening of Crystal Cave.

Unfortunately, Crystal Cave was not the success the family had hoped for. It was too far off the main road for tourists, four and a half miles further than Mammoth, with the only access being an "almost impassable" dirt road.

Besides that, the opening of Crystal came at a bad time. World War I was just coming to a close and the "Spanish Flu" epidemic was just beginning. People weren't traveling as much, and the tourism industry had taken a hit. Cave owners were forced to fight it out over their share of the dwindling tourists, employing whatever tactics they could to lure them in.

Men, known as "cappers," for the hats they wore, would jump up on the running boards of automobiles traveling between Cave City and Mammoth and con travelers into visiting their own caves. The Collins family even took turns scouting the highway for potential tourists to bait. But competing caves were actively dissuading tourists from trekking all the way to Crystal when they could enjoy a much closer and more modern-equipped cave like theirs. The income that Crystal Cave generated wasn't enough to keep the family afloat and they had to continue relying on farming and mining to get by.

Floyd continued to work the family farm, give tours, and sell cave souvenirs to tourists but, as always, his recreational time was spent caving. He was convinced that most of the caves in the area were connected. He searched through over five miles of Crystal's passageways looking for a connection to Mammoth Cave. However, he knew that the real money would be in discovering a new entrance or outside opening into Mammoth Cave. Floyd figured that if he could find one closer to town, off the main road, his cave could become the *first* stop for tourists instead of the last.

Floyd studied the area in detail and came up with a plan to explore a ridge that he thought was the most likely spot for an opening that might connect to both Mammoth and Crystal Caves. He knew of a sand hole on the property of Beesley Doyle which was only 300 yards off Cave City Highway. He began negotiating with Doyle and the other two landowners on the ridge, Edward Estes and Jesse Lee. Floyd

The clogged entrance to Sand Cave after word began to spread that Floyd had become trapped inside.

drove a hard bargain, but he promised that he would find "something big." They agreed that they would split the profits of any cave he found 50/50. The first half going to Floyd and the other split between the three property owners.

Floyd began to examine the hole on Doyle's property that would soon become known as Sand Cave. The name is a bit misleading. It wasn't so much of a cave as it was a deteriorating, narrow crack winding down into the earth. Floyd had to spend the first few weeks clearing out the entrance and digging a crawlway in the crumbling tunnel. Floyd's family was concerned about his current explorations and tried to discourage him from continuing. His father Lee thought he should be more concerned with the failing cave they already had. His brother Homer warned him that it sounded like a "bad 'un" that he might get caught up in it. His stepmother Miss Jane cried and begged him not to go back in after he told her about a disturbing dream he'd had in which he was "trapped by a rockfall and was finally rescued by angels."

Floyd wasn't at all worried about the dangers. He was far more focused on the thrill of adventure, the glorious cavern he was sure to uncover, and the subsequent income that would solve his family's money problems. Floyd had previously used dynamite to clear the remaining obstacles in his way and now he was ready to wriggle past the jagged chunks of broken rock, into the waiting darkness.

It was the morning of January 30, 1925.

The previous days had been full of freezing rain and recent thaws meant the ground was saturated. It would be a cold, wet slog through the mud and rock-filled passages. Before entering, Floyd took off his thick coat and hung it on a rock outside the entrance of the cave. He would need to be as streamlined as possible in order to fit through the tightest squeezes. He went in wearing only a wool shirt, overalls, jumper, and hobnailed boots. *Trapped!* described him at this time as looking, "older than his thirty-seven years, his face appearing gaunt behind a long, sharp nose, deep-set eyes and a prominent gold front tooth." He carried with him only a length of rope and his lantern. This was the last bit of daylight he would see for a long time, but there was no hesitation as he headed down into the cave.

If you look at a cross section of sand cave it looks like an ever narrowing and descending zig-zag of steep angles and vertical drops. The cave's entrance passage is a gently sloping 18 x 24-inch passage with a small hole at the bottom, leading to a 4-foot chute, or drop through, which Floyd lowered himself. The next passage forced him to crawl in the mud on his hands and knees as the path curled underneath itself before narrowing to a tight squeeze that Floyd then had to squirm through. On the other side of the squeeze was a slightly larger passageway that continued downward at a near 10-degree angle before suddenly pinching to another squeeze barely 10 inches high. Floyd would need to crawl his way forward through sharp rocks and mud on elbows and knees.

This led to a small chamber, later known as the "turn around" room that was just big enough for Floyd to sit up in. Here, he had stashed a crowbar, a shovel, and some burlap bags earlier in the week.

From there he moved forward, crawling flat on his belly through several inches of icy water and muck, quickly arriving at the tightest squeeze yet -- a 9-inch gap that led to a "ten-foot pit-like chute" at the bottom of which was "a cubbyhole the size of the inside of a kneehole desk." The way forward was through a crack about the "circumference of a large wastebasket."

He had gotten this far in the cave several times before but couldn't proceed until he'd removed debris. There was so little room at the bottom of this chute that Floyd was forced to work upside down while removing the loose material. Once the way was clear, he slipped himself cautiously into the cubbyhole and through the narrow crevice, checking the stability of the loose rocks in the ceiling as he went. He couldn't help but notice, as he passed under it, that a large, jagged rock "hung ominously" over the narrowest part of the crevice. Past this, he entered onto the ledge of a hole about 60-feet deep. Floyd was excited because the potential of a passage leading to a larger cavern below now seemed assured.

As much as he wanted to explore the hole for further passageways, the sudden flicker of his lantern signaled that it was time to return to the surface. Floyd pushed his lantern ahead of him, as far as his arms would reach into the crevice. Then, he lay on his back and wormed his way forward, "hunching his shoulders, twisting his hips, and pressing his feet against the walls and floors." Floyd had now reached the tightest squeeze of the fissure and again went to shove his lantern ahead of him. This time, it tumbled over into the cubbyhole, plunging him into total darkness.

Floyd didn't panic. He'd been caught without light before. He tucked in his arms and tried to make himself as flat as possible, while once again wriggling his shoulders and hips. He put his feet against what he thought was the cave wall and kicked out for a final push into the cubbyhole.

But his right foot hit the hanging boulder he had so skillfully avoided on the way in.

The rock broke free from the ceiling and fell, pinning Floyd's left foot in a narrow "V-shaped" indentation on the floor. He then kicked out with his right foot, trying to dislodge the rock that was trapping his left foot. But he only succeeded in loosening more rocks which tumbled down around him, further trapping his left foot and then his right.

As *Trapped!* described it:

Floyd's head was lying towards the cave's entrance, just at the cubbyhole in the bottom of the 10-foot chute. He was reclining as if in a barber chair, lying on his left side at an angle of about forty-five degrees. His left arm was partially pinned under him, his left cheek rested against the floor rock, and his right arm and hand were held close to his body by the crevice wall... entirely surrounded by rock and earth, he was in a coffin-like straightjacket.

With his feet and arms pinned in place, he was held immobile, unable to roll over. Floyd was stuck in the pitch dark, 115 feet from the entrance of the cave, and 55-feet underground. Fear gripped him and he panicked. Floyd started frantically tensing and flexing his muscles attempting to wriggle his feet free. With his partially free left hand he dug at the gravel that was accumulating around his legs. Every bit he was able to remove was replaced by even more shifting debris and soon his fingers were raw and bleeding. He violently squirmed his body, twisting and arching his back trying to get free of the sharp stones that poked into him. But every movement caused more sand, gravel, and rock to cascade in around him until he was entirely encased with even his hands stuck in place, completely immobilized by rocks on all sides.

Adding to the troublesome situation, was a stream of cold water running across the boulder above Floyd and steadily dripping onto his face. He knew it was probably useless but what else could he do? Floyd began to scream. He screamed until he lost his voice and passed out from sheer exhaustion. When he woke up, he screamed some more. That was how Floyd would spend the next 24 hours, vacillating between bouts of screaming and fits of sleep.

When Doyle and Estes finally realized that Floyd was missing, they trekked through the icy mud to the entrance of Sand Cave, bringing along Estes' 17-year-old son Jewell. As they approached the entrance to the cave, they saw Floyd's coat hanging outside the cave and became worried.

"FLOYD!" they called out into the darkness. But they received no answer. Lighting a lantern, the trio ducked into the entrance passage still calling out to Floyd as they slowly crept forward. Doyle and Estes only made it as far as the first squeeze and immediately gave up, but young Jewell pressed forward. Jewell had no caving experience, but he was slim and sturdy. As he inched his way forward through the freezing slime he nervously called out into the void of darkness before him, "Floyd! Floyd!" He was about to abandon his search out of fear when he finally heard a soft, rasping voice in reply, "'Come to me, I'm hung up.'"

Jewell tried to push his way forward past the final squeeze, "'Is that you, Floyd?"

"Yep. Bring some tools," Floyd replied. He seemed calm and matter of fact. His main complaint was that he was cold and hungry, but he was sure that he could be freed. Jewell was unable to get through the last squeeze and admitted to Floyd he was too afraid to continue. Floyd urged the frightened boy to hurry out of the cave and bring help.

The first organized rescue party to enter the cave was assembled by the first member of Floyd's family to arrive on scene, his brother, Marshall. Marshall selected a crew from the small crowd of curious neighbors that had already begun gathering at the site and although he didn't have much experience in caving led them into the ground. Of the five men he selected, only one made it with him all the way to Floyd. The others all became stuck or gave up out of sheer terror.

When Marshal finally laid eyes on his brother at the bottom of the 10-foot chute he was shocked. How on earth did he get in there? He tried as hard as he could to fit himself through the final squeeze, but it was no use. Even though he was the smallest of the Collins brothers, he couldn't fit. He attempted to widen the opening with a crowbar, shoveling away loose dirt with his bare hands. After 3 hours without much progress Marshall was overcome with exhaustion and had to exit the cave leaving his brother behind.

Floyd's youngest brother, Homer, didn't find out about the situation until he was heading home from a trip to Louisville in his Model-T and stopped to get gas. Assuming that Homer had already heard the news, the attendant casually asked him if Floyd was out yet. Worried, Homer immediately left for Sand Cave and arrived at the entrance around 4 pm. When he arrived on scene, he was bothered to see men sitting around campfires on the hill above the cave. The heat from the fires causing the snow and ice to melt and seep down into the cave.

Homer was taller than his brother Marshall but of the two of them, he had more caving experience. When he heard that Floyd was still not free, he lit a lantern and without even changing from his city clothes, climbed down into the cave. Sliding his way down the angled passages, he was annoyed to pass by several men who appeared to be standing around doing nothing but smoking and drinking. They just shook their heads "no" when asked if they'd been to see Floyd.

Homer weighed about the same as Floyd, but he still couldn't force his way through the final squeeze. "'Floyd you alright?" he called down the chute.

"That's my old buddy, Homer! I knowed you'd be comin' down to help me!" Floyd cried out.

Homer had to back up to the turnaround room and strip down to his underwear in order to reduce his bulk. Returning to the squeeze, he tried again. This time he was able to work his way through the squeeze and down the steep chute, receiving lots of scrapes and bruises in the process. Once inside the cubbyhole Homer realized with an inward shiver that there was barely enough room for him to crouch. Homer's lantern was handed down to him. He looked around with a mounting sense of horror as he took in the severity of his brother's situation. Immediately a frustrating problem that would vex every rescuer from here on out became apparent.

Trapped! Described the problem like this:

> *"If a person came into the chute head first, he was forced to work upside down and was compelled upon leaving to push himself feet first up the sharp slant and then backpedal 20 feet more before he could turn around. If he dropped in feetfirst as Homer had just done, he could not bring the upper part of his body down to Floyd's level without contorting himself into almost impossible positions."*

Homer contorted himself and began trying to clear away some of the loose rocks from Floyd's shoulders. Using a syrup can to collect them, he handed debris to the other rescuers outside the chute for emptying. Food was brought for Floyd, but because his arms were stuck, Homer had to feed him each bite like a baby. Even so, Floyd scarfed down "nine sausage sandwiches and a pint of coffee." As he ate, Floyd told Homer of the pit he had discovered. He was sure it would lead to the big cave he was looking for. He was already planning his return trip and was thinking about the alternative route he would need to find.

Homer continued to claw at the rocks with his hands until they were shredded and bleeding. He still hadn't made much progress. Like a grain silo, new rocks continually tumbled to take the place of the ones he removed. Homer was tired, frustrated, and cold. When Floyd noticed this, he sent his brother away telling him to send his friend Johnnie Gerald in to help. Before Homer left, he picked up some of the burlap bags Floyd had stashed and covered Floyd's face with them to protect him from the tortuous drip-dripping of water on his face.

Homer emerged shaken by his experience but tried his best to downplay the seriousness of Floyd's situation. He believed they would find a way to get him free. From 8 pm to midnight that Saturday night, a parade of well-meaning would-be rescuers went in and out of Sand Cave. However, none of them made it all the way to Floyd. Most of them turned around when they were overcome with fright or caught up at one of the squeezes. Once free from the constricting, muddy, wet tunnel, none of them was willing to enter again. After his attempt to reach Floyd, Ellis Jones from Cave City declared, "'I wouldn't go back in there for a cold thousand, bad as I need money."

It was sometime after midnight when Homer reentered the cave, bringing with him a piece of oil cloth to shield Floyd from the dripping water. He resumed his excavations with the syrup can being passed back and forth. Homer tried using a crowbar to pick at the shifting gravel and rocks but there was hardly any progress, and the work was going slow. Three more hours of hard labor

had only removed enough debris to uncover Floyd's upper arms and torso. Homer took a break, fed his brother some coffee and milk, and placed a dry blanket over the top of the wet burlap hoping it would help to keep him warm. He resumed the exhausting work until the early hours of Sunday morning when his body began to give out. With tears in his eyes, he left Floyd with a promise to return with some whiskey.

It was 6 o'clock on Sunday morning when Homer finally stepped out of the cave into the daylight after 8 hours of strenuous labor. After all that, Floyd was still buried up to his waist -- it wasn't enough. Homer was beginning to doubt they would never get Floyd out alive at this rate and he still had no plan for how to get the rock off Floyd's foot. Homer was overwhelmed. He could no longer hide his apprehension from those around him and his face conveyed the gravity of the situation.

By now word had gotten out about Floyd's predicament and an increasing number of curious bystanders with no connection to Floyd began to gather on the hillsides. Drinking at the site became common among the onlookers and even some of the rescuers. Although lots of well-intentioned potential rescuers entered the cave, only one group made an organized effort that day to reach poor Floyd. At around 9 am a small team descended into Sand Cave. When they reached the top of the chute, they found Floyd shivering and called up the tunnel for a quilt to be brought forth. One of the men stuffed the quilt down the chute and tucked it around Floyd with his feet. Unable to do anything else, they struck up a conversation with Floyd.

Well-meaning, would-be rescuers rushed to the scene, but no one could get Floyd out. The shaft where Floyd was trapped was so terrifying that many who climbed in to help refused to return.

"'Can't you help yourself, Floyd?" they asked.

"No," was the reply.

"Can't you wiggle your foot and pull it out? Try, Floyd, try!"

"I can't, I tell you. I jes' can't. I'm trapped and trapped for life."

Other men continued trying to reach Floyd but failed. The most any of them could do was shout to him from the top of the chute. By Sunday evening, there were over 100 people gathered outside the entrance to the cave. Most of them had never been in the cave. They stood around and argued back and forth over poorly thought-out methods of extracting Floyd. The few men who were still entering the cave would come back out

looking grim, unable to think of a solution. After Carl Hanson, a veteran Mammoth Cave guide saw it, he announced, "'I've been a-caving for twenty-eight years, and I've never seen anything like it." The rescuers gathered at the site began to feel hopeless.

While Homer was still recuperating from his previous rescue attempt, he managed to persuade some teenage boys to take food in for Floyd. The boys took off into the cave but returned after only a short while telling stories of how they had talked with Floyd, fed, and comforted him. Homer knew they had to be lying. Frustrated with the lack of progress, he prepared to go back in himself. He grabbed the prescription whiskey bottle he had promised Floyd and moved towards the entrance. Unfortunately, the bottle was spotted and confiscated by the recently arrived Cave City magistrate, Clay Turner who had received complaints of public drinking.

It was about 5 p.m. when Homer again wrestled his way through the tunnels to Floyd. Alarmingly, he noticed a few rocks that had been jarred loose from the ceiling by all the pointless coming and going of rescue traffic. Most upsetting of all, he found abandoned food and blankets stuffed into cracks and crevices. It was obvious that despite appearances otherwise, no one had actually been down to see or feed Floyd since Homer had left him that morning. Thankfully, though, Floyd seemed to be in good spirits. Homer resumed digging and after some effort, was able to uncover Floyd's left arm and hand, though they remained pinned to his side.

Homer then used a ball peen hammer and a chisel on the limestone block above Floyd, trying to widen the gap between Floyd and the rock. His efforts were in vain. The tiny tools were no match against the solid limestone. Besides that, pounding on the rock was causing more sand and

gravel to filter down. When Floyd became frightened that the block might come loose and crush him, Homer quickly gave up on the idea. Next, he tried to use a blowtorch, which experiments at the entrance had shown would make the rock brittle. Squatting in the cubbyhole just inches from Floyd, he attempted to light the torch. It wouldn't light. He tried several more times and then that too was abandoned for fear of setting off an explosion.

Once again, he was back to using the syrup can. He desperately dug at the rocks covering his brother's waist and legs, removing gravel bit by bit, until at last he could see Floyd's hands. They were caked with dried blood and dirt, flesh peeling off his fingertips from his initial panicked digging. After four hours of intense physical labor, Homer was utterly spent and had to be helped from the cave.

He collapsed at the nearest campfire where he was met by his brother Marshall who was anxious to know what more they could do for Floyd. Homer was exhausted physically and emotionally. He had no idea what to do. Their father Lee wasn't helping matters. He had started ranting about how "'Floyd's entrapment was God's Will, Floyd might never get out." Marshall was nearly beside himself and suddenly burst forth with a proposal of $500 to anyone in the crowd who could bring Floyd out. No one came forward right away but eventually a man named Clyde Hester stepped forward. Hester gathered a small crew of semi-drunken volunteers and off they went into the cave. Hester was only gone but a few minutes before he returned and declared that Floyd was dead.

The family was shocked and began to cry and pray. Clay Turner, who was also the Cave City Coroner, began to investigate immediately. He recruited a volunteer, L. B. Hooper, to check on Hester's story. Hooper crawled alone through the passageways for nearly half an hour of suspenseful terror. At last, he poked his head through the final squeeze and called down the chute, "Hey Floyd, you there?"

There was silence for an intense few moments, but then a faint voice floated up from the darkness, "I'm hungry. Bring me something to eat."

Floyd was alive! Hester was a liar!

Morale among the rescuers reached a new low point. Floyd had been trapped for two days and although rescuers had meant well, their efforts had been haphazard,

Homer Collins was so exhausted he had nearly be carried out of the cave.

foolhardy, and unorganized. Many of the people on scene were short on caving experience but long on ideas about what should be done, and arguments grew among the factions. By Sunday night, February 1st, many in the crowd were drinking moonshine to steel their nerves before attempting a rescue, to calm their nerves after they had tried, and, most frequently, to stay warm under the steady drench of freezing rainfall. The rain continued past midnight further discouraging the rescuers who now had to crawl through several inches of frigid water standing in some of the passageways.

Now, nobody wanted to volunteer themselves, moonshine or no.

Homer was worn out and discouraged. He felt the only person left he could trust was himself, and so he returned to the cave at 2:30 am and began the arduous crawl through the now water-logged tunnels. When he reached the cubbyhole, he found Floyd's condition appalling. Floyd was shivering violently and complained that he couldn't feel his hands and feet. Homer began to worry about Floyd's body temperature. An average-sized person swimming in 54-degree water would die of hypothermia in just 4 hours. Floyd had now been laying in a small stream of ice water in the chilly air of the cave for two and a half days.

As his mind began to slip, he faded in and out of consciousness. It became difficult for Floyd to tell the difference between his lucid dreams and waking moments. Reality and dreams merged together, and he sometimes thought he could hear unintelligible voices yelling at him.

As time passed Floyd became increasingly delirious. He dreamed feverishly that, "White angels came riding by in white chariots drawn by white horses." When he startled awake and found himself still trapped, he began praying and cried piteously. When he finally noticed that Homer was with him, he began to wax poetic about rich foods and their tantalizing aromas as if he could smell them in the air. He talked about his soft feather bed at home, where he could stretch and change positions. He cried and begged Homer to take him home to his bed and save him some "liver and onions." Homer tried not to think about his brother's ramblings, but Floyd's suffering was heart wrenching to witness. Eventually he stopped working and curled up next to Floyd to provide warmth and keep him company through the night as his tortured mind was wracked with hallucinations.

On the morning of Monday, February 2, Homer had just resurfaced haggard and soaked to the bone from his overnight vigil in the cubbyhole. He was thawing himself by a fire and updating Marshall on Floyd's worsening condition, when a small man stepped up to them. Homer was not in the mood to deal with more of the curiosity seeking crowds he had come to despise.

"I hear you're the brother of the fellow who's trapped in the cave," the man said.

Homer intended to ignore him, but the man proceeded to ask questions. "Are you going to get him out?" the man probed.

Homer was exasperated, "If you want information, there's the hole right over there. You can go down and find out for yourself."

Homer had expected this to be the end of it and was stunned when the man accepted his suggestion and began changing into a pair of coveralls. Homer and Estes agreed to escort him in.

The man was reporter William B. Miller, a petite 21-year-old who was only five foot five and weighed in at a mere 117 pounds, earning him the nickname "Skeets," because he was "no bigger than a mosquito." Originally aspiring to be an opera singer, Skeets, who took a newspaper job as a "police reporter" after high school, didn't think of journalism as his permanent career. In 1925, Skeets was still a junior reporter working for the Louisville *Courier-Journal* when he received the opportunity to cover the biggest story of his life.

Skeets had zero caving experience before entering Sand Cave. As he slithered himself through the passages following Homer's directions an uncontrollable well of fear began to

William "Skeets" Miller

fill the pit of his stomach. The ceiling was laced with sharp rocks of all sizes that looked ready to fall on him at any moment and the floor of the cave was a slimy quagmire. After the first squeeze, Skeets was left to continue on his own with only his flashlight for company. Wriggling on his stomach he wormed his way through the mud. Sweaty from the effort, cold from the slush of mud, icy water, sand, and grit sifting down into his eyes from above, he began to feel utterly alone. He called out into the gloom to Floyd and tried to listen for a response over the pounding of his heart. He heard a garbled moan. Skeets crawled toward the sound when suddenly, he slid down a steep angle and landed on something soft. Horrified, Skeets desperately tried to back out of the chute when he heard another moan.

"You're hurting me," a voice said.

Finally coming to his senses Skeets realized he was standing on Floyd.

Floyd's situation was petrifying, a living nightmare. Skeets fought back waves of nausea as his fight-or-flight instincts tried to kick-in. He did his best to calm himself and attempted to interview Floyd, who was still delirious and swimming in and out of consciousness. All Skeets managed to find out was that his leg was trapped by a boulder, and he was dreadfully cold. He encouraged Floyd to hold out for rescue and mustered himself for the return trip. He found the uphill journey to the surface to be even more physically exhausting than the way down. He had to stop and rest several times, fighting panic attacks the whole way. He couldn't keep his mind away from the thought that he too might become trapped. It was an experience that would haunt Skeets Miller for the rest of his life. He felt profoundly relieved once above ground, but he agonized over having to leave Floyd to his plight.

Skeets hadn't been out of the cave long, when Lieutenant Robert Burdon, an aggressively ambitious police-firefighter from Louisville arrived at the cave site expecting to quickly assess the situation and achieve a rescue. He approached the men standing outside the cave, none of whom seemed to be in charge or know what was happening. Burdon decided he would go see the situation for himself and ignoring protests, ducked into the cave.

Burdon was 6 feet tall, but very slim at only 140 pounds, and he was able to slide down into the chute without much trouble. As he hunched over to get in close to Floyd he was startled at the severity of Floyd's entrapment. He'd never seen anything like it. But after only 10 minutes in the chute, Burdon was sure he had come up with the solution.

"We've got a helluva problem here, but I think we can get you out with a rope… we might pull your foot off," he considered out loud.

Floyd was willing to try anything, agreeing, "Pull my foot off, but get me out."

Burdon's idea was met with resistance and the gathered men argued back and forth over the surest rescue plan. But despite fears that

Floyd's vital organs might rupture, ripping him in two, it was agreed to try the rope. Homer went into town and had a custom harness made to slip over Floyd's shoulders and chest. Homer led the group into the cave, carrying with him ham sandwiches, coffee, a sedative from the doctor, and a bit of whiskey. When they arrived, Floyd was weak, disoriented, and in pain. Thankfully, he seemed to recover some vitality and become more lucid as Homer fed him one bite after another. Homer perspired nervously as he slipped the harness over Floyd's head and attached the 100-foot rope. He handed the rope up the chute to Skeets, who handed the rope to Burdon and on to the other rescuers. With hesitation, Homer gave the go-ahead, and the rope was pulled taut.

As the strain lifted Floyd's body off the rock he began to shriek and wail. "Stop! You'll pull me in two!" he cried.

Seeing Floyd's torment, Homer began to scream for the others to stop, but they continued to pull. He yanked the rope with all his might in the opposite direction and finally the rope went slack. The rope-pull idea was a failure. The crew was so spent from their attempt that they had to be helped from the cave and they collapsed at the entrance.

It seemed like there was only one hope left for Floyd -- his childhood friend, Johnnie Gerald. When Gerald first heard about Floyd's entrapment, he had brushed it off as no big deal. He'd been caving with Floyd many times and knew that he could get himself out of a tight situation. In fact, he had been the one to help Floyd out of a collapse at Crystal Cave only the previous summer. He arrived on scene for the first time on Sunday night and was finally told that Floyd had been asking for him. However, Gerald was turned away from entering the cave because it was thought he was too big to fit.

Gerald left to form his own rescue plan, returning just as Burdon was pushing his rope-pull idea. He was outraged by Burdon and his barbaric, inhumane plan to haul his friend up from the depths. Even though he hadn't stepped foot in the cave yet, the Collins family considered Gerald a lead rescuer. He had his own thoughts about what should be done. First and foremost, he wanted access to the cave limited to protect the passageways from further deterioration. He thought the best plan was to keep Floyd warm and fed while going

After Johnnie Gerald arrived, tarps were stretched over the entrance to keep rain out of the cave - and to keep Floyd as warm and dry as possible while they tried to dig him out.

through the laborious process of digging him out by hand. He was certain that reckless outsiders who were unfamiliar with caving would cause a collapse. Gerald selected a crew of approved rescuers, all of whom were familiar with caving.

It was 8 pm when Gerald entered the cave for the first time. Following Lieutenant Ben L. Wells, a teacher and recent West Point graduate, Gerald muscled his bulk through the first sets of squeezes but became hung up at the last one. Floyd was overjoyed when he heard his friend's voice, if anyone

could get him out, he believed it was Johnnie Gerald. Returning to the surface to gather tools, Gerald came back to the final squeeze and began to chip away at it. After several hours of work with Wells, prying away heavy rocks, and hauling them out, he was able to slide down the shaft to his friend.

He would spend hours scraping away gravel from Floyd's body until he had expanded the gap between Floyd's chest and the limestone block and Floyd could move his upper right leg. Finally, progress was being made, albeit slowly.

Now all that was needed was for someone to remove the gravel from his lower legs and lift the rock trapping his foot. With high hopes they placed a dry blanket over Floyd and returned to the surface for some rest.

At 3 am, Gerald and a small crew resumed their excavations. It was tiring work. Gerald had to stoop and stretch as far as his arms could reach, down and around Floyd's waist to scoop out handfuls of dirt and gravel one at a time, handing rubble up to the others with the syrup can. He was now removing debris from Floyd's thighs and legs. Still, Gerald's size was preventing him from reaching in far enough to get past Floyd's knees. "You're shore hung up, but by God, we'll get you free," Gerald encouraged Floyd.

But as hours passed and he was still trapped, Floyd began to doubt he'd be rescued. He sobbed grievously to Gerald about the whole situation. At one point, he even complained that his gold tooth was hurting him. In just three hours, Gerald and his small crew removed an estimated half-ton of rubble from the squeeze, chute, and cubbyhole. When Gerald's depleted crew crawled back above ground it was 6:30 am on Tuesday, February 3.

There had been some press coverage of Floyd's entrapment in the preceding days but on that Tuesday, his story began headlining newspapers nationwide. The initial coverage had been local and the reporting full of sensationalized inaccuracies, but the tides began to turn after the arrival of Skeets Miller, whose reporting was much more accurate and personal, given that it

As word began to spread about the entrapment of Floyd Collins - "world's greatest cave explorer - a flood of people and newspaper reporters descended on the area.

was written from an eyewitness perspective. The Associated Press immediately sprang into action, widely distributing Skeets' eyewitness account to their partnered newspapers. Eager to cash in on the growing publicity, newspapers from around the country sent their reporters to Sand Cave. A media frenzy ensued. Floyd would stay front page news in many of the nation's leading papers for weeks to come.

As Gerald lay recuperating on a cot by the fire, a group of Louisville stonecutters approached with a plan to survey the cave and then cut away the limestone block above Floyd's head. Floyd's father Lee agreed immediately. But Gerald wasn't about to let some outsiders into the cave and undo all the work he'd already done, not when they were so close to freeing Floyd. He refused to let them in and finally, in exasperation, the stonecutters returned to Louisville. Gerald's attitude spread to the other locals, so when Lieutenant Burdon showed up wanting to drag Floyd out with a fire-hose hoist, the crowd screamed obscenities at him. Gerald heard the commotion and when he saw what was going on he also argued with Burdon. With no support, Burdon finally abandoned the rope-pull plan and Gerald left for Cave City to get some rest.

Just before noon, Henry St. George Tucker Carmichael, superintendent of Kentucky Rock Asphalt Company (KYROC), showed up at the rescue site in his well-worn work clothes. He had heard of Floyd's entrapment from Skeets' article in the Louisville *Courier-Journal* and he wanted to help. It was apparent that there was no one directing the rescue efforts and the work being done was chaotic and ineffective. This insulted his engineering sensibilities, and he immediately began to implement an organized and systematic rescue operation. He tasked his group of 20 KTROC volunteers to clear the rocks from the upper passages and shore the walls with timber. Meanwhile, he began to examine the hillside for a suitable place to sink a rescue shaft. By midafternoon, Carmichael had identified a potential spot to sink the shaft and had seven KYROC drillers at the ready.

Again, the locals were outraged with what they saw as outside interference. Homer forbade Carmichael from drilling, believing that the vibrations from the drill would cause a collapse. Besides, Homer predicted that even if they did start drilling, Floyd would never live long enough to be rescued that way. Grudgingly, Carmichael obliged and agreed to focus all his rescue efforts on the existing passages. Working together for the time being, a "human chain" of KYROC workers and locals labored to clear the tunnels, concentrating on widening the first squeeze.

At around 2:30 pm, three local men wriggled their way back to Floyd. They chatted with him while one of the men, Everett Maddox, attempted to clear the gravel from Floyd's legs. Floyd was desperately lonely. He talked to them about how he became trapped, the big "beautiful" cavern he had found, and the rescuers he had met so far. Floyd even refused the milk they brought him, preferring to keep up the conversation. Eventually, Maddox's lantern flickered, and he had to leave, he spared one last glance at Floyd before climbing up out of the chute.

"Goodbye Floyd," he called down.

"Goodbye," replied Floyd forlornly when he realized they were going. "I'll see you in heaven."

As Maddox's team exited, Skeets was ready to enter and this time he had prepared his own rescue plan. He acquired a string of lights, which he planned to drape along the passages, and brought jacks and other tools to enlarge the walls of the trap and lift the rock off Floyd's foot. Skeets planned to either get Floyd out or stay down there with him, even though the thought of it terrified him.

At 5:30 pm Skeets, followed by Burdon, led a team of 10 men into the cave. Skeets tugged the lights along behind him, noticing for the first time how much debris had built up in the cave. Cigarettes, broken glass, boards, food, and clothing littered the rocks.

Skeets slipped through the last squeeze and into the cubbyhole, lifting a lightbulb to look around. He was amazed to find that the pit had been cleared, he could now move around easily. Floyd's foot was still as stuck as ever, but he could now twist his upper body from side to side and move his arms a bit. The change was impressive, and Skeets felt renewed hope for liberating Floyd. Without hesitation, he got to work removing the gravel from Floyd's legs, this time trying a new technique. He carefully slid his legs on either side of Floyd and pulled himself into the gap between Floyd and the limestone slab above him. If he bent his head to the right, and reached down as far as he could, he was able to scoop handfuls of gravel from around Floyd's left leg. There was barely 6 inches of room between Floyd and the rock above. Dripping with perspiration, Skeets slowly but steadily shoveled away at razor sharp gravel at last freeing Floyd's left knee, though he couldn't reach past the trapped man's calf.

Shivering with cold and fatigue, Skeets sat down to feed Floyd some milk, coffee, and whiskey. In the harsh light, Skeets could see Floyd's four-day beard growth and the pain lines furrowing his face. His deep-set eyes appearing all the more sunken by contrasting shadows. Though glaring, the electric lights were reassuring to both of them, and it gave them a sense of togetherness. Skeets positioned

Floyd Collins

Floyd seemed more lucid than he had been in days, and he poured his heart out to Skeets, revealing his hopes and fears. Floyd started out retelling the tale of his entrapment, followed by fantastical stories of the wonderful cave he'd uncovered. But then his mind turned to the present and he spoke of what it was like to be trapped in the dark and incapable of moving. He recalled how his spirit had soared and then crashed with each failed rescue attempt. He told of how his foot hurt so bad he thought it might fall off and how he sometimes cried or prayed uncontrollably. He confessed that he had thought of death and how things might end. He wasn't afraid, but the waiting was agony. As the interview ende,d Floyd announced, "I'm achin' all over, but my head's clearer now than any time since I been here. I'm still a-prayin' all the time... I believe in heaven. But I know I'm gonna get out. I feel it. Somethin' tells me to be brave, and I'm gonna be."

It was almost 8 pm when Skeets was pulled from the cave entrance. Like the time before, he was flooded with intense relief that he was on the surface, but he couldn't get Floyd's pain stricken face from his mind. He took off his mud-caked overalls and downed some coffee while he

himself so that Floyd's head was on his knee and fed him through a straw. It was in this most intimate and unusual manner that Skeets Miller would conduct the interview that would later earn him a Pulitzer Prize.

discussed the next phase of the plan with Burdon. His idea was to shove a crowbar under the rock trapping Floyd and use a jack to hoist it off his foot.

At 9 pm, a relay team of 13 men entered the cave with Skeets and Burdon at the front, forming the longest human chain of the rescue to pass in the needed tools. Once in the cubbyhole, Skeets assumed the same awkward position from before, straddling Floyd and wedging himself into the gap above him. Skeets had to extend his right hand as far as his arm would reach while Floyd stretched his hands to reach what he could and pass it back to Skeets. It took almost 30 minutes of sustained scratching, but they were finally close to reaching Floyd's ankle. The chain of men lay waiting on their backs and bellies in the muck, soaked and shivering in the chill cave air, until at last Skeets called for the jack.

When the first jack arrived, Skeets discovered it was too big to fit above the crowbar, a second smaller jack also proved to be too large for the space. Lieutenant Burdon suggested that Skeets go up to the surface so he could choose the jack himself. The chain of rescuers crawled above, glad to have a break from the tunnels and

Skeets went into Cave City to find a suitable jack for the job. It seemed like Floyd's escape was imminent and the men prepared excitedly for what everyone hoped would be the final push.

Skeets returned with a small jack that had only a four-inch lift but looked like it would fit between the crowbar and the limestone above. At 10:30 pm, Skeets and Burdon, followed by the rest of the rescue chain clambered into the cave. Frustratingly, the new jack was now too small for the space, so he called for some wood blocks to be sent down. Carefully, he placed them between the crowbar and the jack. Then, holding the stack of blocks together with one hand he attempted to turn the jack screw with the other. The force of the jack caused the crowbar to shift, and the blocks tumbled out. Steadying his shaky hands, he tried again and this time he saw the crowbar move.

"Keep turning fella, it's comin' off!" Floyd shouted.

Anxiously, Skeets continued slowly cranking the jack, with the crowbar moving bit by bit. But their growing hopes were quickly dashed when the blocks once again fell from the crowbar. With no choice but to try again, Skeets ignored the searing pain in his shoulders and back and once again contorted himself into the awkward position necessary for the job. When this attempt was also met with failure, the entire rescue team wanted to cry.

Floyd encouraged his rescuer and with grim resolve, Skeets returned to the task for the next hour. He tried repeatedly to balance the blocks and jack in just the right way for the rock trapping Floyd's foot to be lifted. But each attempt was met with failure.

The thought of stopping now made Skeets' heart ache, but the work had been grueling, and it was more than his body could endure. Before leaving, he placed a bottle of milk nearby and placed a lightbulb wrapped in burlap on Floyd's chest for warmth. Nearly numb with fatigue, his muscles trembling, Skeets could barely get himself out of the cave. Everyone was emotionally and physically spent. Burdon and the other rescuers also had trouble getting out and had to be helped through the squeezes.

The media descended on Skeets and Burdon the moment they stepped foot from the cave. With all eyes on Skeets, he spoke from his heart. He stated that Floyd was in good spirits, feeling more alert than before and believed that they were very close to freeing him. He told of Floyd's incredible bravery, patience and faith in God and assured the crowd that he wouldn't give up on Floyd. Nearby, Burdon also gave interviews, stating bluntly that they would have Floyd out in no time. He warned all other rescuers to stay away from the cave, which was becoming unstable. The ceiling was in danger of crumbling. Burdon indicated that Floyd would only need to spend one more night in the cave and would be rescued by Skeets and himself the next morning.

That Wednesday, February 4, Floyd's story was not only maintaining its front-page status, it was a growing media sensation. For days now, his entrapment had been the top news story on everyone's minds, with many following along with the poor man's plight became invested in the outcome. People from across the country began donating to the cause and volunteering their services. Churches across the country held vigils and prayer services in his honor.

But it wasn't just Floyd the public was interested in. Eager to keep their readers interested, newspapers included photos of Floyd's family and rescuers, too. Of chief interest of course, was Skeets Miller. He was the world's contact with Floyd, simultaneously working as an essential rescuer and an eyewitness reporting the story. Through him the nation came to understand the terribleness of Floyd's situation, the misery of his tormented mind and body, and the terror of confinement that was Sand Cave. Skeets gave the country someone to root for and he became a sort of "national hero" almost overnight.

On February 5, the *Courier-Journal* published a front-page article about Skeets, asserting that, "Cave City is 'Skeets' Crazy." Other reporters looked up to him and sought interviews with Skeets. "The kid has guts!" wrote Tom Killian of the *Chicago Tribune*. To Skeets' credit, he remained modest, reminding everyone that the bravest of all was the still trapped Floyd.

Floyd was feeling utterly hopeless. His whole body hurt, he couldn't feel his left foot, and he was terribly afraid and anxious. Hearing Floyd's despairing sobs, a pair of rescuers that had stayed behind when the human chain resurfaced crawled to him and started a conversation. Floyd wanted to know what they were doing to get him out and where Johnnie Gerald was. They did their best to make him comfortable, assuring him that they were doing all they could and would let Gerald know Floyd was asking for him. As the rescuers turned to leave, Floyd, now feeling that hope for rescue was slim, reportedly asked for a "kiss goodbye." On the way back to the surface, the men happened to look up and notice significant cracks in the ceiling near the chute. Large rocks embedded in the ceiling were starting to droop and some of the sand and gravel was starting to fall.

They described their disturbing find to KYROC superintendent Carmichael immediately upon exiting the cave around 2 am. Troubled by the information, Carmichael recruited a reluctant man named John Gerard to go down and assess the situation. Gerard and another man, Casey Jones, crept into the cave around 2:30 am. Gerard was beyond terrified by the time they reached the turnaround room. He could see that the rocks in the ceiling were coming loose and wanted to get out. But Jones pressed forward, belly crawling under a low hanging bulge in the ceiling about 6 feet from the chute. Asking Floyd if he was alright, Jones slid down the chute and tried to give him some coffee, reassuring him that they would be getting him out, not now, but when they came back.

Gerard, faint with fright, was waiting in the passage when he thought he heard earth shifting above him. He panicked and screamed for Jones; afraid the ceiling was collapsing. Jones, hearing Gerard's frantic shouts, dropped the rest of the coffee and scrambled out of the chute. Not knowing what was happening, Floyd cried after them, "For the love of God get a doctor and have him cut off my leg!"

Gerard was mad with fear, already scurrying out of the tunnels as Jones popped out from under the still sinking bulge in the ceiling. At the turnaround room, he glanced over his shoulder and paled as he saw the opening, he had just come through continuing to shrink.

It looked like the whole ceiling was about to collapse.

The last thing Jones saw before getting himself out was the faint glow of Floyd's lightbulb shining through a small hole. Over his shoulder, Jones could hear Floyd begging him to stay with him as he scrambled to the surface. At 4 am, just hours from what many hoped would be his release and four and a half days into his awful confinement, Floyd was now more trapped than ever.

It was a restless night for the rescuers in their Cave City hotels. Even as exhausted as they were, it was hard to turn their minds away from being trapped in the cave with Floyd. Skeets arrived at Sand Cave at 10 am, shortly after Gerald and Burdon, who informed him of the cave-in. Skeets refused to believe it until he saw the collapse for himself. Carmichael warned that it was too dangerous, but Skeets went in anyway. The passage just before the cave-in was only about 18-inches high by two feet wide. The rubble from the collapse, estimated at four feet thick, was blocking the route to the chute. Although Floyd was unreachable, they could hear him through the cracks in the unsettled debris.

"Come on down, I'm free," Floyd called to him.

Skeets was in disbelief. "Are you sure, Floyd?"

"Come on down n' see," he pleaded.

Miller reminded Floyd of the bottle of milk he'd placed above his head earlier and asked him if he could reach it. Floyd sadly admitted that, no, he couldn't, and he wasn't actually free. Floyd was getting desperate and thought the story might make the rescuers work faster. Nobody wanted to say it, but it seemed like Floyd's salvation might now be impossible.

Around 11:30 am, Skeets shimmied his way through Sand Cave for the last time, hauling in a field telephone to the breakdown area. He placed the phone nearby and began carefully picking at the debris in the collapse. When rocks and stones tumbled from the pile onto his legs, his fear finally overcame his determination, and he abandoned any further digging and got out as fast as he could. Greeted by reporters eager for news, Skeets remained optimistic. He thought rescue was still possible. If someone else would just clear the cave-in, then he could lead a human chain into the cave and finish rescuing Floyd.

When Lieutenant Burdon finally examined the breakdown for himself, he estimated it to be 40 feet from Floyd, a much greater distance than the others had perceived. He also said he heard Floyd's frenzied screams for help and frantic prayers. It sounded like he had finally lost his mind. Burdon felt the cave-in was too perilous to touch and doubted that any method of rescue would be successful. Lieutenant Burdon had done all he could do. For him, the rescue attempt was over.

Johnnie Gerald went in to see the collapse at 5 pm and was angered by what he saw. He had warned everyone that the human chain was too big, that body heat and rubbing of the walls from their movements would cause a cave-in. He blamed the inexperienced efforts of Skeets and Burdon for contributing to the collapse.

By Gerald's estimate the breakdown was more like 14 to 18 feet from Floyd. He discussed ways for removing the block with Carmichael. When Floyd heard them talking, he began to cry out. "Johnnie is that you? Why don't someone come to me?"

Gerald explained that there had been a collapse, but they were working on a plan to get to him. Floyd broke down, praying and sobbing desperately. Unable to stand listening to his childhood friend's heart wrenching pleas any longer, Gerald fled to the surface.

Gerald and Carmichael now teamed up to shore the crumbling walls and attempt to remove debris from the blockage. Time was short. If they were to rescue Floyd, they would have to move fast. Carmichael put out the call for volunteers with a warning, "There's death down there. The walls and ceiling are crumbling. Unless you are determined to take the biggest chance you ever took in your life, tell me now and stay outside."

Carmichael added to those that accepted the risks that it would be their last rescue attempt considering that Floyd had been trapped, half-starved in the cold-wet dark for five days, and surely couldn't last much more.

Men worked for four hours shoring the walls and propping overhangs and rocks with boards and logs. However, they found the passage near the collapse too narrow to work in. Gerald, Maddox, and Wells took turns working at the head of the collapse, reducing the mountain of debris one rock at a time. Gerald and Carmichael finally had an orderly system in place and the locals served as security guards, keeping anyone that wasn't on the approved list from entering the cave. As an outsider, even Skeets was kept from going into the cave. When he tried to enter, Gerald threatened that if he went in now, he probably wouldn't live long enough to get back out.

At 8 pm, Gerald, Maddox, and Wells desperately struck out on their last attempt to get past the breakdown carrying with them cold chisels and a grease gun. They hoped to be able to slather Floyd's ankle with Vaseline

and slip it out from under the rock. Hazardous and laborious work, they battled a cascade of falling rocks until at last they had cleared a small opening. The narrow tunnel through the debris was at risk of collapse at the slightest touch of the sides. A KYROC team did what little they could to shore up the crumbling passage.

Claiming that he would have Floyd above ground within the hour, Johnnie confidently entered the cave with Wells and a chain of four men. Just past the turnaround room, Gerald came upon a second cave-in. Despair and frustration overwhelmed him and he sat down to collect himself before warily picking at the rocks. A small rock fell from above and bounced off his head. He paused apprehensively and called for Floyd. Hearing no answer, he bellowed Floyd's name at the top of his lungs.

"Don't bother me," Floyd groaned, "I've gone home to bed and I'm going to sleep."

When Gerald resumed his frantic digging, a boulder weighing about 40 pounds crashed from the ceiling and hit him in the spine. Terror-stricken, he backed up to Wells, telling him, "I'm done, my nerve's gone."

It was 11:45 pm when the frightened crew reached the cave

entrance. It was obvious to the waiting crowd that the mission had failed. Distraught, Homer was stopped from rushing into the cave. Floyd's father seemed resigned to accept his fate as God's will. Johnnie Gerald confessed to reporters that, "he would not go back in there if he were deeded the whole state of Kentucky. It was suicide to try anything more."

Still, people wanted to try something and so one last attempt was made to reach Floyd via the existing tunnels. Unfortunately, after two hours of work, they hadn't made any progress. Reverend Roy Hyde compared it to "digging in a barrel of apples - remove one, and others fall in."

At 4 am, the dispirited crew exited the cave, declaring it their last trip. No one wanted to continue risking their life with no hope of achieving rescue. The last intelligible words Hyde heard from Floyd were, "You're too slow."

With Johnnie Gerald out of commission, outside engineering experts stepped in to survey Sand Cave's passages and see what could be done. They had been gathering at the site and investigating the situation for days. Survey teams immediately set to work, and a civil engineer named Roy B. Anderson drew up a map. It indicated that Floyd's position, due to the twisting nature of the tunnels, was located 55 to 60 feet underground and 15 feet northeast of the cave entrance. Based on this information, the engineers began looking for a spot to sink a shaft.

At 1:15 am on Thursday, February 5, Kentucky Governor William Fields ordered Lieutenant Governor Henry H. Denhardt, a brigadier general in the national guard, to take over command of Floyd's rescue. Known for his aggressive personality, Denhardt quickly took authority over the site, although his methods clashed with locals' opinions. At 8:30 am, Denhardt officially declared that a shaft would be sunk and that no one would be allowed into the cave without his permission. He put Carmichael in charge of sinking the shaft, offending Homer, who felt sure that the shaft idea was ignorant and would basically abandon his brother to death.

After some argument about the exact placement for the shaft, drilling finally began around 1:30 pm. The work was slow. Worried about exhaust fumes from equipment getting into the cave, they had to resort to digging and hauling everything out by hand. By Thursday night, Carmichael had assembled a team of over 75 experts to

Equipment had originally been set up by engineers to do the heavy digging for the rescue shaft, until locals reminded them that exhaust fumes could get into the cave and kill everyone inside.

began to encounter rocks mixed in with the muck. By 7 pm, they had only dug down seven feet, meaning they were only digging at the rate of one foot per hour. The work was moving at an excruciatingly slow pace. By 2 pm the next day, they had only reached a depth of 15 feet. The two or three workers that could fit in the shaft at one time had to contend with several inches of muddy water in the shaft and large boulders needing to be removed one at a time.

help with every aspect of the work. Load after load, filled with donations of equipment and supplies, began to arrive on site. People sent railroad ties, drills, wheelbarrows, pickaxes, even tractors, and a lighting system. As the work got underway, Carmichael estimated that if they worked around the clock, it would take them 36 hours at a digging rate of two feet per hour to reach Floyd. The numbers were grim. Floyd had already been trapped for 144 hours and he hadn't eaten for the last 36 hours.

The first four or five feet of the shaft were carved out quickly as they consisted mostly of mud. But work slowed in the next few feet as they

Because the sides were continually giving way, work was paused every three feet for shoring with railroad ties. Worried about Floyd, Carmichael tried to find ways of speeding up the process, but to no avail. To make matters worse, the warming weather caused melting snow and ice to flow into the shaft, making it miserable to work in and increasing the threat of cave-ins. By Friday night, with the shaft at 17 feet, Carmichael unhappily revised his estimate for when they would reach Floyd to Sunday at the earliest. "There isn't a chance... but we're going to keep on digging until we find the body," Carmichael told reporters.

On Saturday, February 7, experts offering their services and trucks bringing more supplies than anyone knew what to do with, continued to arrive on site. The surrounding hills were littered with large equipment, wire and cables, sledgehammers and picks, cots and blankets, coffee pots, and campfires. The national guard sent 50 men to guard the rescue site, which they enclosed with a barbed wire fence. The operation was growing so large that the American Red Cross stepped in to defray costs and took over the job of serving coffee and sandwiches to the expanding crowd. The mass of onlookers had ballooned from 500 on Friday to an estimated 2,000 people - all there to watch the excavation of the shaft on Saturday. Groups of the morbid curious had begun to roam around gawking and whispering to each other.

In 1925, Cave City had a population of 680 people and with this influx of reporters and curiosity-seekers, the population quadrupled. Anyone who owned a car became a taxi driver, charging a fare of $1.50 to take someone to Sand Cave. Hotel rooms were completely over-booked, 5 to a room, with cots and mattresses placed in the hallways and some people even

sleeping in bathtubs. At least 150 journalists, photographers, and cameramen swarmed the hotels on Broadway Street, which became the hub for reporters from all over the United States. Cave City's rural phone lines weren't equipped to handle the load and reporters waited in lines for as long as two hours to phone in their stories.

This would all be just a hint of what was to come.

The public was captivated by the Floyd Collins' story. Not only was Skeets' incredible firsthand coverage thrilling to read but Floyd's entrapment took place in the middle of winter, when everyone was shut indoors and had plenty of time to read or listen to the radio. Newspapers around the country were selling out of hundreds of thousands of papers a day. That, combined with the "live" radio updates and dramatic news reels, created the perfect conditions for Floyd's ordeal to become one of the first viral news stories to sweep the nation.

The sea of humanity that surged into the Cave City and Sand Cave area on Sunday, February 8 would be remembered as "Carnival Sunday". The crowd was easily more than anyone in Cave City had ever seen in

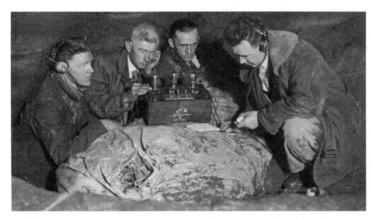

Radio reporters did "live" updates from the scene, which were broadcast all over the United States.

stands and lunch wagons appeared, selling sandwiches, hotdogs, and hamburgers at prices inflated to five times the usual value. Vendors sold postcards, merchandise, and souvenirs to the public. A favorite among the children was a blue balloon painted with the words SAND CAVE.

their whole lives. Estimates put the crowd somewhere between 10,000 and 50,000 people. Excited families came from near and far, traveling by mules, buggies, automobiles, and trains. Lines of near standstill traffic filled the road for over three miles from Cave City and became so bad by midafternoon that state troopers forced people to park their cars and walk the rest of the way. Open fields became parking lots for approximately 3,000 vehicles.

If you were one of the people converging on Sand Cave, you might have thought you were arriving at a festival. Families picnicked on hills, children ran through the mud screaming in delight, men helped giggling flappers over fences and puddles, and jugglers strolled through putting on performances. Souvenir

Floyd's father, Lee, took the opportunity to pass out advertisements for Crystal Cave, telling stories of Floyd's caving explorations and selling Floyd's portrait for $1 each. The throng was also rife with pickpockets, con artists, and moonshiners discreetly hawking their "tonics." The spectacle was so entertaining that people stayed for hours, milling about trying to catch the latest action.

The main event was a service in Floyd's honor given by a Louisville reverend, James A. Hamilton, whose dramatic sermon was heard by an audience of 5,000 men, women, and children, as another 5,000 curious onlookers traipsed about. Hamilton's sermon was rich in symbolism that spoke to the hearts of both the locals and outsiders. With rescue workers, barbed wire, and construction noise from the shaft as his backdrop, he led the congregation in hymns such as "Lead Kindly Light" and especially poignant, "Nearer, My God To Thee." I can't help but wonder if Floyd could hear them singing as he lay dying, encased in the earth deep below their feet.

Sadly, the complications of sinking the shaft seemed never ending. They had to replace the shoring constantly and when they hit a patch of hard rock, work temporarily came to a near standstill. When blasting the rock with dynamite didn't work, they had to chip it away by hand. By 1 pm, the shaft was only just a little more than 23-feet deep. They were progressing at only eight feet a day and it pushed estimates for reaching Floyd all the way into Wednesday. In desperation, they searched for alternative routes into Sand Cave and experimented with pumping harmless banana gas into Sand Cave to see if it could be smelled drifting in any of the other nearby caves. However, nothing was gained by either endeavor.

The sensationalism of Sunday had been speculated upon in the press, leading some to wonder whether Floyd

FLOYD COLLINS TRAPPED IN SAND CAVE

Above is entrance to Sand Cave, near Cave City, Ky., where Floyd Collins, left, was trapped by an eight-ton boulder which dropped from the roof, pinning his foot. Diagram shows how Collins was trapped. Dotted line is where workers hoped to clear space to free Collins until second cave-in sealed cavern. A shaft is being sunk from above to reach the entombed man. Small inset is Jewel Estes, 17 years old, who discovered Collins' plight.

was trapped at all. Perhaps the whole thing was a hoax. Some suggested that Floyd might be sneaking in and out of the cave at night or conversely that rescue was being delayed for profit or maybe he was murdered and dead from the start. A military inquiry would later be opened to investigate the allegations, but other than providing fodder for hungry journalists, not much was uncovered or accomplished there either.

A continuous drizzle started up late Sunday night and as dawn broke on Monday, February 9, a foot of water sat at the bottom of the rescue shaft and a pump was installed to try and keep up with the flooding. The punishing hours digging shifts at the rescue pit grew longer as volunteers -- not wanting to be involved with the military's investigation-- dwindled in number. Morale was lagging and the stream of support and supplies slowed to a trickle. Once the "cave probe" got underway some of the volunteers returned and by 11 pm on Tuesday, the shaft had reached 40 feet. The appearance of cave crickets and the scent of banana gas told them they had to be getting close. Workers guessed the shaft could be as close as 10 feet from connecting with one of Sand Cave's passages.

Wednesday morning's newspapers boldly declared that Floyd Collins would be free by the end of the day.

But oh, how wrong they were.

The rain had turned to snow, and the temperatures had fallen into the twenties. Crews now spent up to four hours at a time in the shaft, straining with frozen hands to keep the walls from giving way. On Thursday, February 12, they again ran into multiple limestone blocks. Using a diamond drill, they probed for openings or cracks but found none and had to resort to breaking the blocks apart with a hammer and chisel. Once they passed 48-feet, the

shaft was more unstable than ever, and multiple cave-ins began causing regular severe delays.

At 10 am on Friday the 13th, a four-foot crevice was discovered at the bottom of the shaft. The dig team was elated when they thought they heard coughing coming from within it. Rumors ran wild and by the time news reached Cave City, it had morphed into claims that Floyd was alive and freed. The press swarmed the area once again, creating so much chaos at the dig site that they had to be cordoned off from the shaft. This welcome boost to the volunteers' morale did nothing to alleviate the problems with the shaft. Sampling with the diamond drill showed there were no more voids below them and a side shaft would have to be tunneled to intersect with Sand Cave's passage. Continuing to six feet before moving sideways, they ran into so much loose debris that portions of the shaft collapsed and had to be shored up continuously.

By 9 am Saturday morning, the shaft had only reached 54-feet and 12 hours later, had only been extended by another foot. Carmichael, noticing that the shaft was increasingly unstable and beginning to slump on one side, ordered reinforcements of the walls and a lateral shaft to be started before it was too late. A thunderstorm passed through between 9:30 and 10 pm, soaking the workers with sheets of icy rain, which flooded the shaft with two feet of water even with the pump running. To satisfy the newsmen, Carmichael brought Skeets down to view the shaft. Unsettled by dropping debris while at the bottom, Skeets reportedly found it to be "five times worse than the hole."

As Sunday, February 15 drew near, Cave City prepared for an even larger crowd than the previous week. However, the crowd that arrived this time was less than half the size of "Carnival Sunday." There were no food vendors or street performers, just copious amounts of mud to trek through. Still, the scene was much the same, with curious families lined up along the barbed-wire fences to view the rescue work.

Meanwhile, the men in the shaft toiled in unimaginable conditions to dig out the lateral shaft, every inch of it had to be shored as they went. By 11 am it was five-feet-long. At 3:30 pm, with the side shaft at seven feet, testing with the diamond drill revealed there was a void six feet ahead and five feet below. When Carmichael updated the press at 10 pm, he predicted that Floyd was only six or

seven feet away, but it would take at least 12 hours to get there.

The whole world was anxious to know, would Floyd be alive when they got there?

The afternoon of Monday, February 16, with the lateral tunnel at 12-and-a-half-feet long, Albert Marshall broke into Sand Cave with a final tap of his chisel. Calling excitedly to alert the others, he pried at the small hole until it was large enough to stick his head in. There Marshall was greeted by "stale air and darkness so thick he could feel it." Marshall was understandably hesitant to enter the cave, so a man named Ed Brenner volunteered. Using his flashlight to examine the scene, Brenner was shocked when his light reflected off something shiny -- it was Floyd's gold tooth.

Apparently, the tunnel had come out in front of and above Floyd's body, not behind him as they had planned for. Brenner saw that Floyd was once again entombed in debris up to his shoulders and his lightbulb had gone out. Floyd's mouth was gaping, his sunken eyes were partially open, and he had a red blotch on his cheek from the constant stream of water flowing onto it.

Floyd Collins was dead.

Doctors that later examined Floyd and declared that his death had been caused by a combination of starvation and exposure and that he had probably perished sometime on Friday the 13th. Floyd's body was still as imprisoned as ever and with conditions in the shaft rapidly deteriorating, the decision was made to leave Floyd where he was and seal the cave.

Floyd Collins' funeral was held near the entrance to Sand Cave at 2:30 pm on Tuesday, February 17. Floyd's family and 150 locals, rescue workers, and reporters gathered to listen to a service by Rev. Roy H. Biser. The service began with a heartfelt singing of "Nearer, My God To Thee." Film cameras were running as the reverend eulogized Floyd. Rev. Biser

Workers pray over the exhumed body of Floyd Collins for this publicity photo, taken at Sand Cave.

concluded by saying, "Floyd Collins' body lies in yonder cave, but his soul is with God." As the 54-minute funeral ended, A.F. Pearson, an undertaker, tossed a piece of ash wood, a fern, and a handful of dirt down the rescue shaft. By the next morning Sand Cave was nearly deserted, save for a few reporters, and by 5 pm the shaft and cave entrance had been sealed with concrete.

But then exactly two months later, on April 17, W. H. Hunt, a man hired by Homer to retrieve his brother's body, broke into the 60-foot cavern Floyd had stumbled upon.

It was definitely *not* beautiful.

But there they found Floyd; his ankle still pinned by that damned rock. It was shaped like a leg of lamb and weighed just 27 pounds. Bee Doyle, Sand Cave's property owner, declared himself the rightful owner of the rock and it would eventually go on display as a tourist attraction -- along with Floyd's shoe -- in the Sand Cave ticket office.

When Floyd was finally brought to the surface on April 23, there were only about 100 people in attendance. Floyd's emaciated body was wrapped in a sheet and raised to the surface on a stretcher. To document the affair, Hunt and his miners posed with Floyd's body for a photograph. After everyone had viewed the remains and identified the corpse as Floyd's, the body was placed in a wicker casket and taken to the morgue in Cave City for embalming. The process took three days, the undertaker had to reconstruct Floyd's ears and parts of his face which had been eaten by cave crickets. He finally received a proper burial on April 26, 1925. He was buried in a grave next to the Collins family's Flint Ridge home, his resting spot marked with a large stalagmite.

A group of tourists pose around Floyd's casket - with his body in clear view through the glass top - in Crystal Cave.

This might have been the end of his story, but this is where Floyd's legend really begins.

In 1927, Floyd's father Lee, hurting for money, sold Crystal Cave for $10,000 to Dr. Harry B. Thomas, a dentist from Horse Cave. He also authorized him to move Floyd's body if he wished. Realizing the tourist potential of having Floyd's corpse on display, Floyd's body was exhumed and placed in a glass topped coffin on Crystal's main concourse. The macabre new feature drew in hundreds of curious tourists, who stood at Floyd's sarcophagus and listened in respectful awe as guides recalled "the world's greatest cave explorer."

Appalled by the exhibition of Floyd's body, his brothers attempted to sue Dr. Thomas for $50,000 dollars, claiming that their father had been manipulated into selling the cave. But the court found the sale to be legal and binding, Floyd would remain enshrined in what became known as Floyd Collins' Crystal Cave.

Or would he?

In the dead of night on March 18, 1929, unknown body snatchers removed Floyd's remains from his

Inside of Crystal Cave, Floyd's casket remained on display, even after the cave was closed to the public in 1961.

casket and took off with them. Floyd's corpse was found the next day not far from Crystal Cave on the banks of the Green River, with the left leg missing. No one was ever charged. While some speculated that Homer might have hired men to retrieve Floyd's body from Crystal, others thought Dr. Thomas might have paid for the body to be stolen to boost tourism. Either way, from that point on Floyd was locked into the cave at night and his glass coffin was enclosed in a metal

case. Still, for the right price, a curious visitor could peek at Floyd through a window in his casket as late as 1952.

In 1961, Floyd Collins Crystal Cave was sold to the government for $285,000,000 and, although closed to the public, it became the focus of intense research into the connections between caves in the karst landscape around Mammoth. After 11 years of exploring the tunnels in Crystal and Mammoth, cavers discovered what Floyd had always insisted was possible. On September 9th, 1972, a team of six, left the Collins Family home on Flint Ridge and after 15 hours of spelunking, emerged onto Mammoth Cave Ridge from the Snowball Dining Room. Dubbed the Flint Mammoth Cave System, it became the longest known cave system in the world with 144.4 miles of labyrinthine passages.

As the decades have passed, Floyd's story seems to have taken on a mythic quality as it's been retold in many forms, from newspapers, music, books, radio, movies, and tour guides to now musicals, podcasts, magazines, and blogs. Floyd's story has all the ingredients for the making of a great legend. His tragic saga is abundant with potent universal symbolism that becomes an allegory for life. His death, confinement, isolation, loneliness, starvation, coldness, and darkness take on a personal meaning as we mentally journey with Floyd into Sand Cave. I think that's one of the reasons why Floyd's tale has such an enduring and haunting legacy. We can all understand and imagine the terror of these things.

After 64 years, Floyd was finally given a permanent resting place on March 24, 1989, at the Mammoth Cave Baptist Church cemetery on Flint Ridge.

But I'm not so sure he rests in peace.

I broke out in goosebumps several times while reading descriptions of Floyd during his entrapment. They sounded an awful lot like the "old" man from my dream who kept repeating that he was "under the rocks." When I looked at a picture of Floyd and imagined what he must have looked like near the end of his entrapment, in the dark, emaciated, with sunken eyes and deep pain lines worn into his face, I realized that image looks very much like the frail man I saw in my dreams. And the "musty, wet stone and earth" smell of his breath? It didn't occur to me 20 years ago, but that's exactly how I might describe the scent of a cave or the underground. Floyd was a

The grave of Floyd Collins today, located in the cemetery for the Mammoth Cave Baptist Church on Flint Ridge.

dreamer. He even foretold his own death in a dream. Could it be possible that Floyd was reaching out to me in dreams for some reason?

When I visited Big Mike's Rock Shop back in October of 2001, I had no idea of its close proximity to Sand Cave, just under one mile -- a two-minute drive away -- down the same highway that rescuers, reporters, and tourists used to get to Floyd's rescue site back in 1925. The antique store I visited on Broadway Street was near where all the hotels filled with reporters, including where Skeets would have stayed. Perhaps Floyd

Collins still wanders the highway looking for tourists to lure into his caves. Or, could there be another more personal aspect at play?

There's one more synchronicity yet to reveal. I thought that I was nearly finished with my article when I began to research Cave City, but I was actually just at the beginning. When I was at the start of learning about Floyd Collins and getting more excited by the minute, I called my Mom up and breathlessly told her how I was planning to write about Floyd. Later that evening, I got a text telling me, "Btw. There is a reporter named William Burke Miller on your family tree that interviewed Floyd Collins." It wasn't until the next morning when I looked him up on my family tree that I realized he wasn't just *a* reporter, it was Skeets! I was reeling with the incredible coincidence. Skeets Miller, the most admirably adventurous of rescuers and reporters, is my first cousin seven times removed. I had no idea! My dad was adopted, so I only just learned about the Miller side of my family earlier this year through a DNA test.

William "Skeets" Miller's life was changed forever by his experiences at Sand Cave. His firsthand reporting won him a Pulitzer Prize in 1926. He was essentially guaranteed a future in journalism and went on to be hired by *New York Morning World* in 1927. Eventually, he switched over to radio and was hired by NBC where in 1931 he was put in charge of their special events programming. Skeets broadcast live radio stories from the most unusual locations and circumstances. He transmitted stories from submarines, dirigibles, lion cages, and even while dropping from the sky by parachute. He was once proclaimed "the bravest man in radio" by Robert Ripley of "Believe It or Not".

Recalling the events of Floyd's entrapment in 1978, Skeets was haunted, wishing he'd thought of some way to hold the blocks together during the jack attempts. He told the authors of *Trapped!*, "I will regret it all my life that we didn't save Collins... It still makes me shiver." William Miller died at the age of 79 in January 1984 in Sebastian, Florida.

I'll never know for sure whether Floyd's story or my relation to Skeets has anything to do with my strange experience in a Cave City hotel room 20 years ago. But I'll certainly never think about the experience the same way again.

CONTRIBUTORS
The Morbid Curious No. 4

AMANDA R. WOOMER

Writer, anthropologist, and former international English teacher, Amanda R. Woomer was born and raised in Buffalo, NY. A member of the Society for Psychical Research, she is a featured writer for the award-winning *Haunted Magazine* and the owner of Spook-Eats. She is the author of *A Haunted Atlas of Western New York, The Spirit Guide: America's Haunted Breweries, Distilleries, and Wineries,* and *The Ghosts of the Ghostlight Theatre* as well as two books in the Creepy Books for Creepy Kids series. She has also begun curating the all-new all-female paranormal journal, *The Feminine Macabre.* Follow her spooky adventures at spookeats.com and on Facebook, Instagram, and Twitter.

SYLVIA SHULTS

Sylvia Shults is the author of *44 Years in Darkness, Fractured Spirits: Hauntings at the Peoria State Hospital,* and other books of true ghost stories. She has spent the past twenty years working in a library, slowly smuggling words out in her pockets day by day to build a book of her own and she sits in dark, spooky, haunted places so you don't have to. After battling an intense, lifelong fear of the dark, Sylvia decided to become a ghost hunter. As a paranormal investigator, she has made many media appearances, including a tiny part in the *Ghost Hunters* episode "Prescription for Fear", about the Peoria State Hospital. She is a recurring guest on Ron Hood's podcast Ron's Amazing Stories, with the monthly segment "Ghost Stories With Sylvia". She is also the writer, director, producer, and host of the true ghost story podcast Lights Out, available on YouTube, iTunes, iHeart Radio, Spotify, and anywhere else great podcasts are found. Sylvia loves hearing from her readers, especially when they have spooky stories of their own to share with her. She can be found at www.sylviashults.wordpress.com and on Facebook at the pages for Fractured Spirits and Ghosts of the Illinois River.

APRIL SLAUGHTER

April is a longtime part of the American Hauntings family, co-author with Troy, and designer of all the book covers for American Hauntings Ink. She is the author of three books and numerous articles on ghosts, hauntings, spirit communication, psychical research, the unexplained, and death and funeral customs. She is also the founder of "Slaughter Skulls" and an accomplished artist. She was born and raised in Utah, where she developed a love for history and genealogy, and currently resides there with her husband and twin daughters.

GINA ARMSTRONG

Gina Armstrong is an author, historian, musician and avid photographer who resides in Maple Ridge, British Columbia. She is co-founder of the award-winning Haunted History BC with her sister, Victoria. Gina belongs to several historical societies and focuses much of her work on preserving and sharing the heritage, folklore and ghost stories of British Columbia. Gina and her sister have published, *Haunted – A Unique Look at BC's Capital, Haunted Vancouver* and most recently, *Dead Things*. Gina is currently working on *Evenings & Avenues – Hauntings in the Outskirts*, a book featuring local history, hauntings and legends. Gina's co-authored essay, Supernatural British Columbia, appears in the recently released *Feminine Macabre Volume II*. Haunted History BC is a current nominee for the BC Museum Association Distinguished Service Award and for the Governor General's History Award to be adjudicated later this year.

You can find Gina on hauntedhistorybc.com, Twitter and on Instagram.

KARI BERGEN

Kari Bergen is an intuitive assemblage artist, lover of strange and unusual history, and owner of the historical oddities shop, Ephemera Obscura. She is a life-long lucid dreamer who has spent the last 20+ years studying the Metaphysical and investigating the Paranormal. She has given talks for Atlas Obscura on topics such as Victorian Mourning, Postmortem Photography, and the History of Disaster Tourism.

You can find Kari at https://ephemeraobscura.com

TROY TAYLOR

Troy is an author of books on ghosts, hauntings, true crime, the unexplained, and the supernatural in America and the editor and creator of "The Morbid Curious." He is also the founder of American Hauntings Ink, which offers books, ghost tours, events, and weekend excursions. He was born and raised in the Midwest and currently divides his time between Illinois and the far-flung reaches of America.

SPECIAL THANKS TO:

April Slaughter

Amanda Woomer

Sylvia Shults

Kari Bergin

Gina Armstrong

Lisa Taylor and Lux

Brianna Snow

Kaylan Schardan

Cody Beck

Lois Taylor

Orrin Taylor

Rene Kruse

Rachael Horath

Elyse and Thomas Reihner

Bethany Horath

Becky Ray

John Winterbauer

Lydia Rhoads

Maggie and Packy Lundholm

Tom and Michelle Bonadurer

Susan Kelly and Amy Bouyear

Cheryl Stamp and Sheryel Williams-Staab

American Hauntings Crew

Made in the USA
Monee, IL
26 April 2022

95462878R00085